Randy

9/4/09

THE PRESENTER'S GUIDE TO BEING PREPARED

52 REAL-LIFE SITUATIONS AND SOLUTIONS TO HELP YOU WIN OVER ANY AUDIENCE, ANYWHERE

by David W. Richardson, CSP

THE PRESENTER'S GUIDE TO BEING PREPARED

52 REAL-LIFE SITUATIONS AND SOLUTIONS TO HELP YOU WIN OVER ANY AUDIENCE, ANYWHERE

by David W. Richardson, CSP

Published by:
Janisue Publishing
10410 E. Cholla
Scottsdale, AZ 85259

www.richspeaking.com
speaking@richspeaking.com

ISBN: 0-9708281-2-8
Printed in the United States of America

DEDICATION

This book is dedicated to my granddaughter
Riley Claire Woodyard

TESTIMONIALS

"I have always been amazed by the fact that the fundamentals, not major issues, create problems in business and life. In his new book, David answers many of the questions most of us are too embarrassed to ask, but to which most of us need the answers. The book will serve as a valuable resource to anyone in a leadership role."

Terry W. Chandler
President/CEO
Diamond Council of America

"What a relief to realize you're not the only one with jitters and speaking frustrations! Dave Richardson makes you see that everyone's in the same boat . . . but reading 'The Presenter's Guide to Being Prepared' give you some excellent 'oars'!"

David L. Lloyd, Jr.
Vice President & General Counsel
GE Aircraft Engines

"Dave Richardson has hit the mark. This book is an easy to understand reference guide anyone can use to improve their presentations."

Tom Kuzma
President
Nautilus Insurance Group

"Speaking before a group of people—the #1 fear we continually strive to conquer. The Presenter's Guide is guaranteed to help anyone become a more confident presenter."

Tony Vottima
Vice President/General Manager
Avnet Hall-Mark

TABLE OF CONTENTS

INTRODUCTION

"Dave, I nailed it . . . I knocked 'em dead . . . I blew 'em away!"

"Everybody came up afterward to tell me how much they had gained from my speech." . . . "One person approached me to ask if I could speak at an upcoming college commencement."

"That's the second straight debate where the polls declared me the winner." . . .

"I've never felt such a strong connection with my congregation." . . . "This was one of our biggest projects ever; you pushed us all very hard, but we won the bid."

"Even in light of our poor showing in the market, the board of directors was actually optimistic and will support almost every one of our proposals."

This is what it's all about . . . the words that make it all worthwhile. A CEO, company president, engineer, project manager, pastor, sales manager, or a politician, each achieving a newfound excellence on the speaking platform.

Whether it's one on one speech coaching, an intense presentation skills workshop, team coaching, or the origination and design of a message, the pride in their voices or the look on their faces when they finally "get it" is only exceeded by that special moment when they have just nailed it.

My work is so rewarding because, somewhat like a physician, people come to me with problems of varying degrees (in my case, their skill in delivering and designing a presentation). Early in the process they recognize that our work together is more than just one speech or one presentation . . . it is a lifetime change in how they communicate to the world.

Many of the corporate people who have participated in my coaching have been promoted; many are now presidents and CEOs of growing businesses. Politicians have been elected. Architects, construction contractors, engineers, and electrical firms have won coveted multi-million dollar projects. Pastors have made a more powerful connection with their congregations.

Along the way, the underlying questions from my clients were what if this happens, what if I forget that, etc., etc. So here I have categorized these "what if" situations along with real-life stories and numerous easy-to-use solutions. I believe you'll benefit from these insights as my clients have.

Got a presentation coming up? Check out your "what if" in this book then throw the book in your briefcase for continued reference whenever or wherever you make a presentation or speech.

David W. Richardson, CSP

1

WHAT IF I'M PETRIFIED EVERY TIME I'M ASKED TO SPEAK?

THE SITUATION

Early in my career I hated to speak; in fact, I was absolutely petrified! On a scale of 1 to 10, my fear level was 11.5! Whenever I was asked to make a presentation, I would eagerly say, "When?" Then if they answered, "Wednesday", I would respond, "Sorry. Tuesday or Thursday would be okay, but I'm busy on Wednesday."

Having just been promoted to regional sales manager, I was told I would be making a presentation at a management meeting in Chicago. The morning of the meeting I sat in my hotel room looking at the airline guide, planning to leave, to go back home to Connecticut because I didn't want to embarrass myself by giving this presentation.

Somehow, though, my feet took me to the meeting room and I delivered my presentation. Guess what? It was a disaster! Making my way back to my seat, I purposely avoided the eyes of the 25 managers and executives in the room.

Several minutes later, seated in my chair, feeling an odd sensation of dampness, I glanced down and discovered to my horror that the front of my trousers was soaking wet from the waist down. I have no idea what had happened, but I knew that when I ultimately stood up, I would be faced with a further element of monumental embarrassment.

So I did what any petrified, fear-mongering speaker would do: I poured a glass of water and set it near the edge of the table. Now I was ready. As the speaker who followed me very eloquently delivered a humorous line, I "accidentally" tipped the glass and lavishly spilled the water all over my lap. Brushing my pants, I jumped up and muttered these words, forever etched in my memory, "You klutz!"

Excusing myself, I walked to my room, and as I did, I swore to myself, "This will never happen to me again. I will either learn how to do this or I'll become a garbage man where I never have to speak to anyone again."

THE SOLUTION

As someone who has been there, I can tell you first-hand that being absolutely petrified to speak is real, and if not aggressively addressed can sabotage your career. You must take hard action:

1. Attend a presentation skills workshop, minimum two days, taught by an instructor who has been where you are today, someone who understands what it means to "be petrified". Someone who has always been a good speaker and trainer simply can't identify with the depth of fear you are desperately trying to overcome. If possible, attend this workshop with your peers, your direct reports, or people from your company, and then watch not only the growth that takes place, but the synergy that develops within the group.

2. Engage a professional speech coach, but again, make sure you carefully interview that person to ensure you work with a pro who has "been there, done that".

3. Join Toastmasters International. Here you will meet a caring group of people who are working to overcome similar fears as yours.

4. Once you've begun this process, volunteer anywhere you can practice this skill, such as your church or a local school.

5. Do you really want to see how well you're doing? Videotape one of your presentations and watch it with an open mind.

Because I was highly motivated, I diligently followed all of the suggestions listed above. As a result, I became a strong business speaker. Few people are born to be speakers, but this is, without a doubt, a skill that can be learned.

CHAPTER 2

WHAT IF I CAN'T GET MY PRESENTATION ORGANIZED?

THE SITUATION

I had to make a presentation. I knew basically what I wanted to say, how much time I had to say it, and who the audience was, but when I sat down to write it, bullet-sized beads of perspiration popped out on my forehead. I got my glass of water, then arranged everything carefully on my desk, preparing to write my message.

Typing it would have been great, but my dyslexia and my typing teacher, whom I seriously disliked because she continually intercepted notes between my girlfriend and myself, strongly suggested that typing should not be part of my high school curriculum, so typing was out.

Sitting down to write my speech, I had to first refill my water glass, make a telephone call, then wander outside in the front yard to see what all the commotion was. It was just two birds chattering back and forth at each other. Normally I wouldn't have noticed it, but on a day like today I noticed everything but the pen on my desk and how it should fit snugly in my hand to write on the pad in front of me.

No flashes of brilliance but, no problem. I still had a couple of days. So I did the only thing the designer of a presentation could do: I went out and played golf. And, best of all, I put that old presentation completely out of my mind – that is until I putted out on the eighteenth hole and a chill ran down my spine as visions of my desk began to dance tauntingly in my head.

Procrastination reigned. I went home, had dinner, and watched a horrible movie that even under the worst conditions I would have normally bypassed. But I still had another day.

Focusing on the impossible, something like writing a presentation, was definitely not one of my favorite things to do. So, in the end, I jotted down a few notes, a few things I might say, and went on to deliver a presentation, or should I say, went on to wing it. And because it was so utterly forgettable, I don't even want to remember it.

THE SOLUTION

We've all had to develop a presentation, and I'm sure many of you have gone through the same painful procrastination I went through. Winging the presentation simply won't cut it.

So, when we sit down to begin to design a presentation, what's the first thing we do? Well, of course, we write the opening, and then the body of the presentation, and then hope we have some pearls of wisdom in our conclusion that supersede "thank you". Right? Wrong!

Try designing your presentation backwards. It makes sense:

1. Determine your objective. When you finish your presentation, how will your audience be different? What specific action will they take? What do you want them to do? Once you have identified the objective, everything else will fall into place.

2. Write an ending that ties into the objective. Here's where you write the final three or four persuasive sentences to encourage your listeners to take a desired action. This may involve the completion of a contract or the signing of an order, or it may be an intermediate step in the process, such as setting up an additional meeting with others in the group or something as simple as getting together again to review some basic procedures, etc. While the long range objective may be to secure a signed contract, the

objective of this meeting may be nothing more than a preliminary session to pave the way for the big meeting.

3. Develop your three or four major points. These are the key areas around which your presentation will be designed and delivered. Use three, four, or maybe five key points . . . never more. Picture this: standing in front of the group, the presenter says, "The 76 points I'd like to talk about today are . . ." Not only do all of the participants look at their watches to see just how long it might take to cover 76 points, but more importantly, they are painfully aware that this is going to be a long one and desperately seek ways to occupy these eternal moments in their lives.

4. Determine the ways in which you will support and validate your message. What are the examples, anecdotes, stories, testimonials, or case studies you plan to use to help your listeners better understand the concepts of your message? People learn by example; they do not learn by the technical, conceptual information you deliver. These can be either business or non-business examples, but they must obviously tie in to your message.

5. Prepare your opening. This is where you develop a creative, "grabber" opening to get the immediate attention of your listeners. Let them know that this presentation is important and you plan to hold their attention.

6. Design your supporting visuals. Here's where you design visual aids that will support your presentation.

7. Assemble your final notes. This does not mean to draft out your entire presentation but to write down some points that will jog your memory. Perhaps, in a different color, jot down a few words that will remind you about the story or anecdote you plan to use.

Now when you sit down at your desk to organize your presentation, you have a road map. By designing it backwards, your presentation will quickly evolve right before your eyes.

CHAPTER
3

WHAT IF I'D RATHER JUST WING IT?

THE SITUATION

The CEO of a large healthcare company was scheduled to be one of the featured speakers at the annual meeting of the National Association of Chain Drug Stores (NACDS). He and his company were involved in a number of challenging, complicated internal events which were gobbling up most of his time. One CEO perk: you don't have to write your own speeches. You can staff that chore out to someone else, which he did.

When offered an opportunity to practice, he declined: "No time. I've done this before, no problem. I'll look it over on the airplane."

Huddling up with his staff members on the airplane, he quickly found other issues to discuss and the speech once again took a back seat. To his credit, he briefly looked it over just before retiring in the wee hours of the morning, five and a half hours before he was to deliver it. By his own admission, he sat there and went through the speech page by page but his mind was miles away.

The next day he walked to the stage, stood behind the lectern, and then the fun began. First of all the teleprompter wasn't working properly but no problem, he still had his entire speech right in front of him. He launched into his speech and then the inevitable happened: he began to stumble over words he was not familiar with. Not the words exactly, but the context in which they were written. Becoming extremely uncomfortable, he began to perspire profusely.

Rather than continue to go down with a sinking ship, he jumped off message and began to ad lib. He was actually quite good, delivering a very meaningful message but totally confused the poor guy who was desperately trying to operate the PowerPoint™ projector in sync with his boss's presentation.

The presentation went downhill from there and he retired from the stage to the polite applause of a somewhat confused audience.

THE SOLUTION

It only takes one speech to torpedo a frustrated, overworked CEO, and this was the one. His company was going through some tough times, so was he, and this was just another nail in his coffin. Arrogance and ego, neither of which are bad in an appropriate situation, caused him to fail on that day. The arrogance that told him, "I've done it before, I can do it again" and an ego that challenged him to do other "more important" things than practice the speech.

Very few people can pick up a speech for the first time and deliver it with impact, energy, and imagination. Even the big guys, even the news readers, memorable names such as Tom Brokaw, Peter Jennings, Dan Rather, and even Walter Cronkite, never sat in their anchor chair cold. Before they went "on" they frequently practiced the entire script not once, but two or three times.

Even some of the presidents who are known for their oratorical skills, Bill Clinton, Ronald Reagan, John F. Kennedy, and Franklin D. Roosevelt, did not step behind a lectern without at least one or two strong practice sessions under their belt. They couldn't afford not to practice and neither can you.

Here are some of the excuses people give for not practicing:

1. If I practice, the material will become stale and old. Perhaps the word stale should be replaced with the word familiar: the material will become familiar to you, which is essential to help you deliver it with confidence and passion. And the only thing that's going to get old and stale is you as you stand up there fumbling and bumbling your way through a presentation. When you're

finished, I guarantee you'll feel a lot older!

2. I don't have time to practice; I'm too busy. Everybody's busy but good speakers make the time to practice. They recognize that if they don't practice and if they don't come across at their absolute best, not only will their listeners suffer but so may their careers. And then they won't be busy any more; they'll have lots of time to practice.

3. I feel uncomfortable when I practice. You must seek and find your "practice comfort zone". Personally, I can't practice a presentation in front of a mirror or in front of members of my family. One of my favorite spots to practice is out in the Arizona desert. There's this one spot on a big flat rock, looking out over seven large saguaro cacti. Standing on that rock I can look them in the eye, use my gestures for emphasis, and feel real comfortable as I practice my speech. And I never fail to get a standing ovation. (Well, I don't know about the ovation, but they are standing!)

4. I stumble and stammer and can't get my timing when I practice. I'm much better in front of a live audience. When I was rehearsing for the finals in the World Championship of Public Speaking, I could not get the speech to come together. I stumbled and stammered, and as I was practicing the delivery I was thinking about everything else but the speech itself. What that told me was that I wasn't ready and I ended up rehearsing that seven and a half minute speech more than

100 times so I could literally say it in my sleep. I've never spent that much time practicing a speech since, but then I've never had to give another speech that was so precise and in a competitive environment. In that presentation I was focusing on myself rather than on my audience. I was completely focused on winning the contest. Now when I practice, my focus is on my listeners and it's amazing how much easier and more effective my practice sessions are.

If the message has value, if it is really worth delivering, then it's worth practicing . . . not for you, but for your listeners.

CHAPTER

CHAPTER
4

WHAT IF I WANT TO USE A DRAMATIC OPENING?

THE SITUATION

Speaking before a thousand store managers from Kay Jewelers, the CEO completed my introduction. As he was returning to his seat I stopped him. Asking to borrow a cigarette and a match from someone in the audience, I lit the cigarette.

I complimented the CEO on his excellent taste in clothing, then asked him to remove his suit jacket. With smoke rising from the cigarette in one hand and his jacket in the other, I said to the audience, "Wool burns a real nice, smooth, even hole. Polyester just melts. And, of course, touch this cigarette to a piece of silk and it goes 'poof'!"

Following a few humorous one liners, I held up the cigarette and directly inserted it into the back of his jacket. Jumping down from the platform, I walked through the audience talking about smoking jackets and blazers as curls of smoke clearly rose from the back of the jacket. The looks on their faces showed confusion and disbelief.

Returning to the stage and holding the jacket high so everyone could see it, I used my right thumb to grind the cigarette into the back of the jacket. Allowing a few seconds for reality to set in, I slowly opened the jacket and amazingly revealed that, not only had the cigarette disappeared, but there was no hole in the back of the jacket!

After returning the jacket to the CEO and thanking him, I immediately launched into my message about taking risks, not being afraid to fail, and accepting challenges with renewed commitment. The presentation was an overwhelming success and achieved our objective: sending managers back to their stores highly motivated and enthusiastic to take charge of their business despite a rather sluggish economy.

Three days later the CEO concluded the conference by recapping the significant events, then shocked everyone by asking one of the regional vice presidents to join him on the platform. Taking the vice president's suit jacket, the CEO proceeded to insert a lit cigarette into the back of the jacket. As he pushed the cigarette into the jacket with his thumb, all of a sudden, without any warning, his entire hand, fist, and arm pierced the jacket. To roars of laughter, the regional vice president donned his jacket, turned his back to the audience, and revealed a huge hole directly in the center. The CEO concluded by saying, "We've learned a lot in the past few days. And I guess if we're going to make it work we've got to go back and put it all into practice."

THE SOLUTION

"Thank you for inviting me here"; "I'm pleased to be here"; tired, unenthusiastic openings that have been overused and abused for many years. Open your presentation by grabbing the attention of your listeners.

1. Magic. I have always liked magic – it's easy to do and makes a powerful point.
2. A story. Tell a dramatic or powerful story that has relevance to your message.
3. Ask a question. Get people involved. Ask a question; acknowledge those who raise their hands.
4. Money. Crumble up and toss aside a borrowed one dollar bill as you talk about throwing away profits and future opportunities.
5. Props. Standing on a chair, pour water from a pitcher into a glass on the floor, saying something like: "A lot of companies are taking long shots and missing the mark. Today we're going to talk about taking short shots, hitting the mark every time."
6. State the obvious. Call attention to something that everybody knows about. Perhaps it's snowing outside or traffic was heavier or lighter than usual.

7. Common experience. Open by talking about an experience you share with one or more people in the group. This might be following a golf tournament at your meeting or an anecdote about the company softball game. I'll open occasionally with a story about building a complicated swingset for my daughters, which is self revealing and humorous.

8. Current relevant topic. A popular sporting event such as the Super Bowl, the World Series, or the Olympics, offer interesting anecdotes to use when opening a presentation. It must be current, within one week of the event. Old news is typically forgotten news.

9. Get the audience to do something. Get them to participate by giving them a short riddle or quick quiz, and draw the answers out from the group.

Creative openings that grab the attention of the listeners are great, but you must plan, prepare, and practice numerous times before actually delivering them. Botching up a dramatic opening might throw you off for your entire presentation.

Great openings are limited only by your creative ability to develop and use them. You have 20 seconds to grab the attention of your listeners – use that time well.

CHAPTER
5

WHAT IF I FORGET AN IMPORTANT POINT?

THE SITUATION

As part of the audience, I was watching a young man as he went through his presentation point by point by point. Part way through point number five he suddenly stopped and explained that he had failed to mention something important during point number two, so he jumped back to point number two. That's when we started to get confused. This added information from point number two was totally irrelevant to what he had been discussing in point number five. Two or three minutes later, without warning, he jumped forward to point number five and continued his presentation.

The majority of the audience was completely lost somewhere between point number five and point number two and then point number five again. Because of this, many people gave up trying to follow his presentation.

Me, I was hungry, so I started thinking about lunch, which quite frankly turned out to be much better than the speech.

THE SOLUTION

People will attempt to follow your presentation as long as your thoughts remain consistent from sentence to sentence, paragraph to paragraph, and point to point. The moment you try to retrieve something forgotten, though, you run the risk of losing the entire group. Here are ways to overcome a forgotten point:

1. Forget it. It's forgotten, in the past; continue on.
2. Work it back into your message and they'll never know it. After all, and I can't emphasize this enough, only you know where the presentation is going.
3. Don't tell them you accidentally left something out. Sometimes we're challenged to follow even the best presentations; admitting a miscue will only confuse your audience and possibly lose them entirely.

Everyone leaves something out of a presentation periodically. It's not what you leave out that counts, it's how you recover.

6

WHAT IF MY MOUTH GOES DRY?

THE SITUATION

While delivering a keynote address to a sales force of 500, all of a sudden, with no warning, my mouth went dry. The more I talked the drier my mouth became. My tongue felt like a swollen balloon, and instead of focusing on my audience, my concentration kept jumping to my dry mouth.

The water glass I had so carefully placed nearby before the presentation had mysteriously disappeared. Continuing to speak, I casually wandered to the front table, looked down and, as I made my point, caught the eye of one participant and subtly gestured to an empty glass. He got my message and poured without a doubt the best glass of water I had ever tasted.

THE SOLUTION

While you can always recover like I did, take time before your speech to do the following:

1. Pour two glasses of water (no ice) and place them where they can be easily reached during your presentation. (And make sure someone doesn't walk away with them!)

2. As a reminder, write the word "water" at the top of your notes or on a small scrap of paper and tape it to the corner of your laptop.

3. Drink from a water glass rather than from a water bottle. Don't laugh; I've seen it done! Why? Fiddling with the cap as you take it on and off will distract your listeners from your message.

4. Drink nothing hot or cold before or during your presentation. You don't want to shock your vocal cords and cause your mouth to get dry more quickly.

5. Use honey and lemon in combination to soothe your throat prior to your presentation.

6. If you're in a critical situation with no water available, place small bits of balled up paper between your gum and your cheek. This will help you produce more saliva.

7. To avoid licking your lips (a signal of thirst), place lip balm or Vaseline on your lips before speaking.

What causes dry mouth? Who knows! With a little bit of pre-planning, who cares? The problem becomes non-existent.

7

WHAT IF MY MESSAGE IS LOST IN THE "LAND OF AH'S"?

THE SITUATION

During my days as a college student, my philosophy professor delivered his 50-minute lecture using only one sentence. Well, what I mean is that every single sentence was connected with the word "ah". The more we heard him speak, the more this non-word, "ah", screamed out at us, completely overwhelming his presentations. He was truly stuck in the "land of ah's".

Philosophy was clearly a pretty boring class. To amuse ourselves, prior to each class we would each write down on a sheet of paper the number of "ah's" we predicted that the professor would utter during his lecture. We placed our written projection along with a $1 bill in an old shoe box. One elected person counted the "ah's" during the 50-minute lecture.

Not being one to fully trust the accuracy of the "ah" counter, I personally counted each "ah" in every lecture. I got a D minus in Philosophy but won several $40 cash pools, and, as a kid in college, that $40 went a long way, particularly on a party weekend!

THE SOLUTION

Non-words such as "ah", "er", "um", "ya' know", "okay", and "like", among others, can be a serious detraction from your presentation. Because the non-words are repeated over and over and over again, the focus of the listener can be seriously deflected from the point you are trying to make.

Using non-words over and over again is nothing more than another way to overcome nervousness. Non-words are frequently used to fill in the spaces between sentences, paragraphs, thoughts, and ideas. We are uncomfortable during the silence so we quickly fill it with an "ah", "er", or "um". Here are some tips for getting yourself out of the "land of ah's":

1. Sometimes what you don't say has a more powerful impact that what you do say. Try pausing at the end of a powerful statement for two or

three seconds, look at your audience and allow them to fully digest what you have just said, and then move on. A brief pause not only forces people to listen to you, but, more importantly, it adds powerful impact to your message that no words can.

2. Audio or videotape your presentation, then during the playback listen for how you use non-words. Most people have no idea that "ah" is such a prominent word in their presentations until they go through the shocking experience of seeing and hearing themselves speak.

3. Try an exercise we use in basic and advanced presentation skills workshops. Stand in front of your peers, co-workers, or, in our case, the participants in our class and deliver your previous presentation. No notes, no visuals, just get up and start talking. Each time you use the word "ah", everyone lobs a crumpled piece of paper at you. The startling reality of paper missiles being hurled at you from all directions is such a powerful experience that you will instantly become aware of the non-words and you'll begin to drop them from your vocabulary.

A partner in a public accounting firm who had attended our advanced presentation skills workshop wrote me six months after the workshop to say that this was the single most self-revealing exercise he had ever participated in, and that "ah" was no longer a word in his vocabulary.

If you want to be a strong, respected presenter, you must take action to drop these unnecessary non-words from your vocabulary. If you don't use them in one-on-one communication, then why telegraph your nervousness when speaking before a group?

8

WHAT IF I DON'T KNOW WHAT TO DO WITH MY HANDS?

THE SITUATION

I was asked to do a media critique of a high-ranking politician's speech as he announced his candidacy for the office of President of the United States. While he was a better than average speaker, on this particular occasion he appeared a little stiff and perhaps too well choreographed.

He had rehearsed his speech so many times that every facial expression, every pause, every gesture was perfectly timed. Or was it? On several occasions, his hand gestures were inconsistent with what he was saying at that moment.

For example, if he said, "We must make some changes now", a natural closed fist, downward-moving hand gesture would normally be delivered at the precise moment the word "now" was passionately uttered. Instead, his closed fist gesture came one complete second after he had finished the word "now".

It's all about timing. His well rehearsed presentation and deliberate gestures were simply out of sync, and, as a result, his message fell short of its mark.

The real essence of my critique: do we want leaders who demonstrate their convictions through great passion, empathy, and feeling, or do we want leaders who deliver words well-crafted by their handlers in order to maximize political popularity in the polls?

THE SOLUTION

Even the greatest professional speakers do not rehearse and choreograph every single move in their presentation. The only people whose words and moves are rightfully tightly planned and executed are actors.

The question I am most frequently asked is, "What do I do with my hands?" Check out some of the ideas below:

1. Let the gestures flow. Quick movements distract an audience. At one time I was a staccato gesturer with short, quick movements. One might have likened me to a director of a John Phillip Sousa march. Fortunately, one of my early speech coaches gave me a very good tip. Gesture smoothly, like a ballerina. Today whenever I'm

making a presentation, that suggestion is implanted in the back of my mind.

2. Emphasize important points. When you add a non-verbal dimension to your presentation, your voice will be stronger because the physical action strengthens the flow of air from your lungs. It will also impact your tone, tempo, and pacing.

3. Focus on your ideas. Many people are visual learners; that is, they draw pictures in their minds as you speak. Appropriate gestures will help them see these pictures more clearly and understand your premise more effectively.

4. Appear strong and natural. Keep all gestures in your upper body (above the waist). Gestures in the lower body are lost to the audience and totally useless. Lower body gestures may make you look like a "flapper" as your hands flop to your sides.

5. Do not hide your hands behind your back or place them in your pockets. These gestures will demonstrate nervousness and could challenge your listeners to question your genuine knowledge of the subject or your interest in them.

6. Use open hands. Don't close your hands into fists as this will appear defensive rather than open and friendly. Don't point at people or straighten your elbows as this portrays a feeling of harshness to your audience. Two-handed gestures add a special punch and a real passion to your presentation.

7. Avoid touching parts of your body or bringing your hands together. Unless done to make a specific presentation point, bringing your hands together promotes playing with rings, cracking knuckles, or just rubbing your hands together.

Gestures add genuine vitality to your presentation by helping you reach out and connect with your audience. Be natural and be yourself.

CHAPTER
9

WHAT IF I WANT TO HOLD SOMETHING IN MY HANDS?

THE SITUATION

A highly-respected senior engineer was conducting a presentation to one of his company's most high profile clients. He was a little nervous, it showed, but he was working his way through the presentation as well as he could.

He was carefully drawing the complex systems he was explaining on a large whiteboard in the front of the room. He held on to that magic marker like my daughter used to hold on to her favorite blanket. He would not let go.

At times, as he gestured, the pen waved back and forth in the air. It kind of reminded me of my music teacher as he directed our high school band.

Then he began to play with it, taking the cap off then putting it back on. Off, on, off, on, off, on. As he put the cap back on, occasionally he missed, and after a few minutes he had almost as much ink on his hand as he did on the board. When he noticed this, he also noticed that we noticed, and everyone shared a chuckle. Very sheepishly, he held his hand up and said, "Oops" and then forced himself to put the pen down.

THE SOLUTION

"Oops!" Instead of paying attention to the speaker we were fixated on not only the opening and closing of the pen but the decorative art being crafted on his hand. Here are a few things to watch for:

1. Whether it's a magic marker, a laser pointer, or a remote control, use it for its purpose and then put it down. You are the centerpiece of your presentation and any extraneous object held in your hand will potentially draw the focus of your audience away from you.

2. Many people tell me "I feel more comfortable if I can hold something in my hand." I watch all of the newscasters and commentators on the major programs and each is holding a pen in his or her hand. They will tell you that, should they need to make a quick note, the pen needs to be easily

accessible. True, but as one sports announcer once told me, "I do feel more comfortable with something in my hand, particularly since it's no longer a football."

3. Personally, if I'm using a marking pen or wireless remote, I find it most effective to stick it in my pocket when I'm not using it, lest I should lose it by absentmindedly forgetting where I put it down.

There are enough distractions during the course of your presentation as it is. Don't add any more.

10

WHAT IF I LOSE MY PLACE?

THE SITUATION

One of my clients, a well-respected attorney from a prestigious law firm, shared with me a defining moment from one of his presentations. While delivering a well thought out and rehearsed presentation to secure a highly sought after six figure contract with a large company, about ten minutes into his message he completely lost his place. Stumbling and stammering, he confessed to the group that he had lost his place along with it his train of thought.

He says, "I recovered in less than a minute, but it seemed like hours. I immediately sensed that I had gained the sympathy of the management team, but that's not what I was there for. At that moment, my firm went from being perceived as a powerful problem solver in challenging times to a weak, lackluster, out of touch legal group. I finished strong, but we didn't win the contract."

THE SOLUTION

Many highly-skilled, very professional organizations fail to win new business contracts because of similar incidents in major presentations. It never has to happen to you if you:

1. Don't admit that you've lost your place or train of thought. You want action, not sympathy.
2. Repeat what you've just said. This should help you jump right back on track.
3. Stop, compose yourself, and move on – only you know where the presentation is going.
4. Ask a question. In a small group, if the time is right, a dialogue may be appropriate and give you time to recover.

Everyone loses their place and with greater frequency than audiences realize . . . they simply recover without obviously breaking stride. It's not what happens to you, it's how you react to it that matters.

11

WHAT IF I START TO RAMBLE?

THE SITUATION

A pastor who is not only a client but also a good friend constantly catches himself rambling about topics both related and unrelated to his sermon. He is an excellent speaker who scripts 90 percent of his message in detail in an attempt to control his rambling. When he gets rolling, though, his exceptionally active mind kicks into high gear and frequently he wanders off on a tangent.

It's not that his congregation walks away with any less value; in fact, usually they leave with a lot more, but he often finds himself in a race against time to thoroughly make each of the points he's planned to cover. This is a concern for him, because it causes him to rush and then he feels that his message to the congregation occasionally comes up a bit short. Because he is such a good speaker, they don't notice it, and, more importantly, they don't care. But he does. He sees rambling as an impediment to achieving his evangelical objective. And he's right.

THE SOLUTION

First of all, there is a significant distinction between rambling and jumping off message in order to interject a relevant new thought during your presentation. People ramble for a variety of reasons. Some are not comfortable with the information they've prepared. Others use it as a means of controlling nervousness, while still others, like the pastor, get brilliant ideas and tend to jump off the message to share them with their listeners.

To control a tendency to ramble, you should:

1. Prepare your presentation (don't memorize it), know what you're going to say, and then say it.

2. If you are prone to "brilliant ideas" during your presentation, anticipate this by leaving some additional time for these "pearls of wisdom". You don't want to get stuck rushing to your conclusion.

3. Rambling is often an attempt to mask nervousness. Approach your objective with confidence and focus on the value the listeners will get from your message.

I am not suggesting that you never depart from your prepared message. Actually, there are several situations in which you must alter your approach. If you feel you are losing your audience it may be necessary to make a change. Someone may ask a tough question or you may feel an overwhelming need to explain a specific concept in greater depth. In situations like these, you should alter your message slightly.

To limit rambling, prepare, practice, know what you want to say and then say it with conviction.

12

WHAT IF MY NOTES GET MIXED UP?

THE SITUATION

The commencement speaker at my daughter's high school graduation was a well-known local personality. Approaching the microphone, this gentleman with a reputation as a strong communicator reached into his pocket and pulled out a stack of 3 x 5 cards that must have been at least an inch thick. These were his notes, and given the fact that he had a lot of cards and obviously a lot of notes, we knew what we were in for . . . a lotta' message.

It was a blustery day in late May, causing several of the seniors' graduation caps to ever so subtly lift off of their heads like kites. And they weren't the only ones feeling the effects of the wind. The speaker was struggling to keep his stack of note cards in place on the lectern. What happened next was inevitable . . . we could all see it coming. The perfect gust of wind lifted his stack of cards into the air, giving those in the front rows the feeling that they were watching a tickertape parade in New York City.

And guess what he had failed to do? Number them. He was totally lost without his notes, and I felt sorry for him as he stumbled through the remainder of his presentation in an awkward, disjointed manner.

THE SOLUTION

While it is highly unlikely that your notes would ever be blown off a lectern, or for that matter somehow become mixed up, plan for the best but prepare for the worst.

1. In this gentleman's case, simply numbering the cards would have helped when it came time to put them back in order, all of which still would have had a negative and time-consuming impact on his message.

2. If you choose to use note cards, use no more than three or four, listing just the key points you wish to discuss so that you present to the audience and not to your notes. People are willing to listen to someone with a couple of note cards in their hand, but 20 or 30 or a large sheaf of papers taken from your pocket clearly sends the wrong message before you've uttered your first word.

3. You may not need notes if you're using visual aids. Merely pick up your thoughts and ideas as you direct your audience's attention to each supporting visual.

4. Practice the entire presentation including the delivery of the message itself as well as the use of your notes in an organized fashion during each rehearsal.

5. People who read presentations often appear to be more interested in what they are saying than what the listeners are getting. As much as you can, don't read your presentation.

Remember that the presentation takes place in the mind of the listeners, not in the voice or the notes of the speaker. Unless you are giving a scripted presentation to a group of earnest listeners who will quote your every word in the Wall Street Journal, a reminder of your key points is all that is necessary.

13

WHAT IF SOMEONE ASKS A QUESTION I CAN'T ANSWER?

THE SITUATION

The selling cycle for a major piece of capital equipment to a hospital was in its fourteenth month. While the typical cycle to close the sale was twelve to eighteen months, this particular client required a lot of hand holding and continuous meetings to keep this project from being delayed or postponed. Even the most seasoned sales professional would certainly find this part of the process frustrating, but by putting it in perspective he would recognize it as just another necessary part of the job.

During one of these meetings with the CEO, administrator, chief of surgery, and the purchasing agent, someone asked a tough but reasonable question. Not knowing the answer, but impatient to bring this sale to conclusion, the sales representative bluffed, made up an answer he felt would satisfy them. It was a good answer . . . but as luck would have it, or should I say, bad luck, the answer was not good enough.

The hospital staff discovered a few days later that by answering this one question, the salesman had not only misrepresented the product but his company and himself as well. His impatience in one brief moment cast a dark shadow of doubt on everything he had ever said. All conversations on this project were immediately terminated. The proposal went back on the market for bid, and neither this gentleman nor his company was invited to participate.

THE SOLUTION

As long as you are honest and up front with people, they will work with you because it's also in their best interests to develop a relationship in which each participant can be counted on without any reservation.

Tough questions . . . expect to get them and be prepared to act, not react:

1. Throw the question back to the group. During seminars I'm occasionally asked questions to which I sometimes don't have the best response. By asking the group I get them to participate, to give their thoughts and opinions, and in most

cases we arrive at a workable solution. Such an approach, however, may not be completely appropriate in all business presentations.

2. Admit that you do not have all the data at your fingertips to completely respond to the question. You might say, "That's a good question. I don't have all the information with me that I need to answer it completely. What I would like to suggest, if it's fine with you, is that I get back to you with the answer (by e-mail, fax, telephone, etc.) before 4:30 this afternoon. Would that be O.K.?" If you've established a good relationship, this type of response should be acceptable. Just make sure you get back to them by the specified time.

Recognize that some day, some time, from somewhere, you will be asked a question and, alas, you lack the appropriate information to give an acceptable answer. As a long-time member of the Boy Scouts of America, I have never forgotten their motto . . . BE PREPARED! That simple but profound motto has helped me numerous times in my career as a professional speaker. Keep your integrity above water. Don't bluff.

14

WHAT IF I DREAD Q&A?

THE SITUATION

A highly-competent human resource manager was delivering a presentation in which she was admittedly nervous and apprehensive during the early portion of the presentation. She told me afterward that her legs were shaking and her palms were perspiring.

All of a sudden, out of the blue, someone asked her a question. She was surprised. She hadn't expected the question, but as she began to respond all the nervous tension in her body drained away. Answering the question in a clear and concise manner, she went on to complete the presentation comfortably and confidently.

THE SOLUTION

We all have a classic case of "I wonder if my audience will like me?" prompting nervousness and concern. Someone asking a question validated the fact that the listeners were interested in what she had to say, thereby significantly increasing her comfort level.

An innocent-sounding adversary, the question and answer period has destroyed many great presentations. Those 15 minutes can make or break the previous hour, yet few presenters know how (or even whether) to prepare for them.

Here are a few pointers for making the most of your listeners' questions:

1. React to the question. While the audience member is asking the question, look directly at him or her and nod your head when appropriate. This encourages the questioner and lets the audience know that you are listening – and that the communication channels are open.

2. Let the questioner finish. It is simple courtesy to respond only after the questioner has finished, so resist the temptation to jump in, even if you know the answer right away (this is not a game show). In case of a long-winded questioner, don't let yourself get caught in a machine-gun barrage of questions from a single individual; answer the first question, then move on.

3. Rephrase the question. Restating the question in your own words before you answer it offers two advantages: it makes sure that everyone in your

audience has heard the question and it gives you time to develop your response. Your paraphrase can also clarify a confusing question or diffuse a loaded one; you can then answer the question you want to answer, not the potentially hostile question being thrown at you. One tip: never answer a question until you clearly understand it.

4. Respond to everyone. This is perhaps the most overlooked area of Q&A strategy, but it is key. While it's true you're getting a question from an individual, remember that this individual represents the entire audience. As you respond, start by establishing eye contact with the questioner, then look at and speak to everyone in the group. As you conclude your answer, look at the questioner again.

5. Refer to the central theme of the presentation. The question and answer period is an excellent time to reinforce your key points. If your response can be enhanced by referring back to a visual aid from your presentation, bring it back up. Repetition enhances retention, so make sure you use every opportunity (within reason) to restate your ideas.

6. Respect the questioner. If your listener asks a good question, say so. If he or she has a different viewpoint from yours, disagree without becoming disagreeable. Diplomacy is essential here. Never, ever ridicule a questioner even under extreme provocation; this will turn the entire audience against you.

7. Feel free to postpone an answer. Sometimes you won't know the answer to a question. In that case, offer to research it and follow up with the audience member at a later date. Then do it. Do not under any circumstances try to bluff! Your bluff may well be called, and you'll be found out in a lie – which will destroy any credibility you've built up with your listeners.

8. Throw the question back to the group. Another way to field a question to which you don't know the answer is to give the question back to the audience, "Anybody here have a thought they would like to share?" Remember, though, that there are several potential pitfalls here. Someone might take the ball and launch into a speech of his or her own, or you simply might lose control of the ensuing discussion. Counteract these developments by making sure you're still the referee: summarize any points made by audience members, then tie them back into your presentation.

9. Validate your answer. When people ask questions, it may be because they (and probably other listeners) have missed a key point or because they simply don't understand that part of what you said. By supporting your answer with an example, analogy, or story, you'll give them a new way into the same material. People often learn more by example than through technical data.

I tell my clients, "When it comes to Q&A, expect the worst and be prepared." A few years back, loaded questions from the audience were rare; today, however, all bets are off. Sooner or later, someone is going to blindside you with a question from left field, and everyone in the audience will be watching to see how you handle it. Most of them are going to identify with the person asking the question, not with you.

Although it's natural to face the unknown with sweaty palms and shaky knees, it's important to remember that a typical Q&A session offers many good things as well – the chance to reinforce your main points, to clarify any misunderstandings, and, perhaps, to gather additional information. Make this valuable time period work for you.

15

WHAT IF MY TECHNICAL PRESENTATION IS JUST PLAIN BORING?

THE SITUATION

Getting a favorable nod following completion of the Request for Quote (RFQ) phase of a major project, two partners in an architectural firm began to develop the oral presentation they would deliver. They would be competing with three firms for this extremely lucrative contract.

The big day finally arrived. In the client's conference room, besides the two partners and one technical associate, were the following members of the selection committee: the division president, the director of engineering, a project manager, the purchasing director and the vice president of marketing.

The presentation itself was well thought out and delivered with great passion and energy. They were extremely thorough. Had this been a committee of architects or structural engineers, it probably would have been a real winner. But you had the president of the organization, who was a finance guy; the vice president of marketing, a sales-oriented person; and the purchasing director, who was probably somewhere between the highly technical and the non-technical listeners in the room.

They failed to win the contract. The prize went instead to another competitor. During the debriefing process, the client was very up front with the partners in the firm. It wasn't that the technical concepts were not well presented; they were. The firm who won the contract explained the technical concepts in "non-technical" terminology.

THE SOLUTION

The architects made the critical mistake of using industry jargon in their presentation, jargon clearly not understood by the decision makers.

In your own professional field, you are continually surrounded by those who speak the same language.

Attorneys use their "legalese" language; engineers, accountants, quality control personnel, computer professionals, and many others use words and phrases specific to their industry. Ever had a doctor try to explain your medical condition to you? You want to shout, "Hey doc! How about telling me in plain English?"

As you read this, pause for a moment to reflect on the terminology specific to your industry. How would you use those words and phrases with individuals who do not share a similar understanding of your profession?

Therein lies one of the biggest challenges in business today. An engineer speaks to a group of venture capitalists; an attorney, on behalf of a client, speaks to the Planning & Zoning Commission; a realtor speaks to a prospective home buyer. Many people choose not to make a decision favorable to the presenter because they don't feel comfortable and often don't fully understand the message.

Here are some excellent strategies to use when presenting technical information to non-technical listeners:

1. Determine the objective of your message. When your presentation is over, how do you want your listeners to be different? What actions will they take? And how will they benefit by those actions? Write out this objective in one sentence. I can't emphasize this enough. If you don't know what final outcome you desire, you might as well not give the presentation.

2. Describe policies, techniques, strategies, concepts, and ideas in terminology that the listener

can understand. This does not mean you can't use technical or complex terms. But when you do, be sure to use an example, analogy, metaphor, or story to help the listener make the connection between what they already know and the information you wish to give them.

People are quickly bored by the technical facts you so ably lay before them. You know very well what it means while they have no clue. Therefore, it's important to validate your technical concepts by comparing them to something your listeners are already familiar with.

For example, you might say, "This turbine is activated through an ignition process with a magnetic reactor . . ." ("Huh?") You've just lost half your audience unless you help them understand what that statement means. To validate that statement, you might add, "That would be similar to our scouting days when you'll remember we used flint and steel to produce a spark that would ignite the dry leaves we had so carefully placed in a wind-protected area."

They may not understand the exact technical process, but now they can make a mental connection to the ideas you're presenting. People learn by example, by grasping the relationship between two completely unrelated concepts.

3. Tell stories. I have a client who is one of the top Six Sigma (a quality control initiative) managers in his company. Called upon to make a presentation to the chairman, president, and other key

executive staff members, he blew it. The presentation was nothing but a technical core dump.

Acting on my suggestion to find stories and analogies to illustrate his points, his presentations now are one illustrative story after another. He is sought after as a speaker not only for his own organization, but also by clients, suppliers, and other manufacturers. Listeners who do not share his knowledge of the specific process have no real interest in the details of how that process works. But tell them what was discovered, what the results were, and the overall cost savings derived, and they're hanging on every word.

Next I suggested that he attempt to insert some humor into his presentations because when people laugh they learn. I recommended that he become more aware of the portions of his presentation that were already creating laughter and then examine ways to embellish and draw out the situation. Further, I suggested that he pick up on the one-liners that were thrown out by people in the audience and find ways to incorporate them into the presentation.

Examine the ways you can tell a story and give your listeners something powerful to walk away with.

4. The rejection committee. When competing for a project with other highly-qualified rivals, recognize that the selection committee is not necessarily trying to choose the best qualified, but rather are screening out the least qualified. Typically,

this decision comes in the form of an intangible, gut-level feeling. The one left standing is usually the winner.

If your presentation is worth giving, then deliver it in a manner that will compel your listeners to take the action you desire. Be a bore no more!

16

WHAT IF I HEAR A GOOD STORY AND WANT TO USE IT?

THE SITUATION

Very, very early in my career I would listen intently to speakers as they told these passionate, motivational stories about their lives. "Wow! These are such great stories," I thought. "Boy, have I ever lived a dull life." I wasn't "lucky" enough to have grown up in a family of 12 children with one parent and living below the poverty level. Nor had I had the "pleasure" of being confined as a POW for almost six years, and somehow I'd missed being in a serious automobile accident, nearly burning half to death, forcing me to speak from a wheelchair. No such luck . . . my life had been a real snore.

I wasn't about to let a little detail like my background deter me, so I began to use some of the material from others and quickly found that I could tell some of these stories myself.

One day after completing my presentation to resounding applause from the audience, the inevitable happened. One of the executives in the audience approached me and said, "Say, let me ask you a question. Was it possible that I heard Zig Ziglar use several of the examples you used in your speech?" As much as I hated to, I owned up to it, and to his credit, rather than admonishing me, he continued by saying, "Dave, you're an extremely good speaker, one of the best I've ever heard. You only diminish yourself and your reputation by using other people's material." Thanking him, I walked away.

Several years later I wrote him a letter thanking him once again, most of all for helping me to build my integrity so that I could not only talk the talk, but walk the walk.

THE SOLUTION

Many high-profile professional and business speakers have had their intellectual property, their proprietary material, stolen and used by others. Jeannie Robertson, one of my favorite humorists, has a trademark baton twirling story which is being told, in some cases almost verbatim, by other speakers.

A highly creative and popular speaker, Joel Weldon, during his presentations says, "Success comes in cans, not cannots" and then proceeds to give everyone a can with those words printed on it. What a great idea . . . but not if you're just copying what Joel created.

Using stories the right way can potentially enhance your presentation:

1. At the conclusion of a well-told story, you have your listeners' undivided attention for at least the next seven to ten sentences. Use that precious time to tie the story into the point you are trying to make.

2. When you tell a story about yourself, about an incident in your life, they will listen because your story becomes their story, particularly if it's self-revealing. Sneaking out to smoke cigarettes as a 12 year old boy, my friend and I accidentally burned up a two-acre field, burned down a barn, and almost burned down a house before the fire department arrived and successfully extinguished the blaze. When I tell that story, people identify with it and embrace it because they almost certainly have a similar story in their background. They may not have burned down a barn, but I will guarantee you something of that nature has happened to them, and for that reason they will hang on every word you say.

3. Tell your own story. To tell someone else's not only opens you up to potential criticism, it's also downright unethical.

4. So you've led a safe, healthy, dull life . . . around which you can create a great story. We all have these stories; we've just got to remember them.

Go to a quiet place, take a pad of paper and a pen, and go back through your life, carefully looking for those forgettable moments when you were embarrassed or humiliated. At the time the pain was so great that you couldn't bear to think about the incident much less laugh about it, but today these events are actually quite humorous. We've all got them. They're actually pretty simple, self-revealing stories. But, it's not a 20-minute project . . . it's more like a 20-hour project. Some of these life changing experiences are buried so deep that finding them could be a great challenge.

Attending my first dance after three months of forced dance lessons, I finally asked the most beautiful girl in the place to dance. And she said, "No". It literally took years to recall the details of that story and another year or two before I could tell it. It's now crafted into a story loaded with humor and passion, and because it focuses on dealing with rejection, it causes my audience to look within themselves and come to grips with opportunities to help them grow both personally and professionally.

Pick up a newspaper and read any of the front page lead articles, or how about the three columns on the front page of the Wall Street Journal. Notice how they are crafted in the format of a story. People love stories, not stories that hammer on how great a person is, but those that demonstrate that even in the face of great adversity the hero overcomes and is a winner.

17

WHAT IF I TELL A JOKE AND NO ONE LAUGHS?

THE SITUATION

As the closing keynote speaker at a two-day international convention of manufacturers and dealers in the sewing machine and fabric industry, my goal had been to arrive early to attend some of the sessions and the trade show. By doing this, my message summarizes the events of the previous two days and sends the delegates away energized, motivated, and with a plan they can use immediately upon returning to their businesses.

During his opening keynote address, the speaker told a joke which was clean, politically correct, and, best of all, elicited a huge laugh from the audience. I couldn't believe my ears when, after the luncheon speaker, another highly recognized professional, told the same joke. The audience reaction: several groans and a few laughs from those who missed the morning keynote.

Unbelievable! Then the opening speaker on the second day told the same joke. After delivering the punch line, he looked up and smiled, prepared to share an uproarious laugh with the audience . . . a laugh that never came. He turned every shade of red imaginable! He also was so thrown off by this totally unexpected audience reaction that he never recovered. And, to top it off, his stories and analogies that followed got little reaction from a highly skeptical and very disappointed audience.

THE SOLUTION

My closing keynote . . . well, you can bet I didn't tell that joke. But about 15 minutes into the presentation when I really had the audience "with me", I said, "By the way, have you heard the one about . . .?" I paused, got a big laugh, then followed up with the critical need to develop your own unique position in your marketplace.

Here are some tips for preventing what might be potentially a serious blow to your well thought out presentation:

1. If no one laughs, pretend you were serious and move on. Don't let this situation wreck your entire presentation.

2. Avoid telling jokes unless you are a humorist or a comedian. If you have heard the joke, it's a strong possibility that others have heard it too. With the availability of so many other great presentation enhancement tools, why take the risk of a failed joke?

3. Even though your joke may seem harmless and politically correct, you always run the risk that someone will be offended. The last thing you want to do is offend someone in your audience whose decision to take the action you desire at the conclusion of your message could be impeded.

4. The humor that we're constantly looking to inject into our presentations comes in many ways. Quite often this is in the form of a one-liner, frequently delivered quite unexpectedly by one of the members of your audience. Look at the ways you can capitalize on that precious moment by following with a funny one-liner of your own.

5. Find the humor in real life stories to make your points as opposed to jokes. People would much rather hear an interesting personal (and even self revealing) story about you to help make your point more clearly.

If you do tell a joke, make sure that it's in good taste and, most importantly, that it ties into the message you are delivering. A pointless joke or a story adds no value and could detract from your message.

CHAPTER
18

WHAT IF I LOSE MY MOMENTUM AT THE END?

THE SITUATION

It was a sad day. Our heavy-duty photocopier, seriously overworked and underpaid, gave up and died. And just to let us know that this was a terminal situation, its painful last breath was in the form of a belligerent clunk.

Buying new office equipment has always been one of my least favorite projects, but we went about the task of researching the market and then invited several photocopier companies in to demonstrate their equipment. If there is a fun part to all of this process, it's observing the sales representatives in action as they make their presentations.

One guy set up a flip card presentation that had so much information on it that it was impossible to follow what the heck it was all about. Amazingly, another virtually read his presentation, giving 20 percent eye contact to us and 80 percent to his notes.

One guy showed up with his district manager and was so nervous during the initial parts of his presentation that his manager jumped in and took over.

Then there was the guy who opened up by asking us questions about our business, the market we serve, the changes we had witnessed, and some of the challenges facing us in the coming months. He made a good presentation using stories, examples, and analogies to clarify some of the more technical points, answered our questions, and then asked for the order.

Complimenting him on his presentation, I indicated that we were in the process of checking out a number of photocopying solutions. He then asked what the criteria for decision making would be and suggested that without trying to bug us he would follow up with us by telephone in two days.

He had a good product and presented it well, and rather than just saying "thank you" and leaving, he suggested next steps, followed through, and got the order.

THE SOLUTION

In a persuasive presentation, your final words should invoke your desired belief or action in your listeners and leave them with a strong final impression. Here are several powerful ending approaches:

1. A simple, straightforward appeal for an action or belief, often after the summary of the main presentation points.

    Example: "Incorporating these ideas and strategies into your business plan will help you achieve your objectives this year and further maximize your profits. After you have had a chance to review the program, we will contact you next Friday to finalize the project."

2. Summary. Summary is always needed, but the quality of this ending is even more important if your speech or presentation is more informative in intent. Repetition aids retention significantly. If you develop four main points, for example, restate the headline of each and tie them all together.

    Example: "In summary, let me state that several legal issues are currently being overlooked by the management team and our company. To ensure that we protect our intellectual property and are in compliance with all issues, please contact me prior to any key decisions in this area."

3. A reference to your introduction. For example, if you described a problem in your introduction and developed a solution to the problem in the body, refer to the original story in your ending. This gives the presentation an appealing unity for your listeners.

Example: "What would happen if your computer crashed in the middle of your presentation? Would you be prepared or would you be pitied? By having backup visuals, or the ability to speak freely without them, you will be able to climb any unexpected hurdles."

Finally: always memorize your ending before you begin. If you ramble or shift ideas in the middle of your presentation, your finish will be weak and ineffective.

With a carefully planned ending, you will close your presentation with brevity, clarity, and confidence and your listeners will be with you all the way. Most important, they will have all the information in an organized format supported by a strong close that will impact the utilization of your ideas.

19

WHAT IF MY TIME IS CUT SHORT?

THE SITUATION

I had been booked by AT&T as the closing speaker at a meeting held in Pinehurst, North Carolina, the golf capital of the world. My scheduled time was 11 a.m. to 11:45 a.m. The first tee time for the group was 12:10, and they still had to go to their rooms, get their clubs, pick up a box lunch, and be ready to play 25 minutes after my presentation. Believe me, I was critically aware of the timing at this meeting.

The division vice-president was scheduled to speak from 10 a.m. to 11 a.m., a one-hour presentation. Fifty-five minutes into his presentation, and still going strong, it was pretty obvious that there was no way he would finish by 11 a.m. And he sure didn't!

As a matter of fact, he kept going. Now it's 11:20 a.m. and I am already well into calculating the pieces of my message I must delete in order to squash my presentation from 45 minutes to 15 or 20 minutes. I was well aware that if I went one minute past my deadline I would lose my audience mentally; two minutes and I would lose them physically, so I was prepared.

All of a sudden an envelope was handed to me. The note inside said, "My sincere apologies – here's your check. We'd like you to come back and speak at our next meeting."

I returned, not to Pinehurst, but to New Jersey during one of the worst snowstorms in history. On this day, I probably could have gone on for two or three hours because the audience loved the presentation and they weren't going anywhere anyway! The nice part: they presented me with a second check and we created a relationship that continues today.

THE SOLUTION

The best solution: always be ready for anything. Be aware of where you can, if necessary, cut 10 percent,15 percent, even 25 percent of your material without trashing your message. If that can't be done, reschedule.

1. If you find yourself running out of time, don't rush and don't start speaking faster in order to "get it all in". Better you cut something out than leave your audience behind in a race to the finish.

2. When performing emergency surgery on your presentation, if you cut out a story or example, remember to delete the fundamental key point. But beware: don't cut valuable support material to the point where your presentation is nothing more than a jumble of boring facts.

3. Perform extensive surgery and you may kill the presentation. Suggest rescheduling to a future time when your message will be more meaningful to the group.

With some forethought and planning it's not impossible to present your information in a powerful and compelling fashion even if you do have to cut it short. And, regardless of what happens, never, never, never exceed the time allotted for your presentation.

20

WHAT IF I'M UNCOMFORTABLE USING A MICROPHONE?

THE SITUATION

How many times have you been at a fairly large meeting or event when a speaker declined to use the microphone? The meeting planner who was to introduce my speech at a convention was such an individual.

To ensure the right introduction, and because it leads directly into what I am going to say, I had given the meeting planner an easy to read, typewritten sheet with large letters printed at the top, "Introduction of

David W. Richardson, CSP. Please read exactly as written." Delivered properly, this introduction perfectly tees up my opening and immediately grabs the interest and attention of everyone in the audience. To my chagrin, the meeting planner pushed the microphone aside saying, "I don't like microphones. I don't like the sound of my voice on a microphone, so I'm not going to use it." And then he launched into my introduction.

I doubt that anyone beyond the first ten rows heard what he said. I walked to the platform knowing that, with the exception of reading the promotion piece in the convention brochure, the majority of the people had no idea who I was. It wasn't the way I wanted it to happen, but it wasn't a serious problem. I merely changed my opening few sentences and jumped into the presentation as though nothing had happened.

At the end, when he was to close the session by suggesting that people step to the back of the room and look at my continuing education materials, nobody heard him! Since this was part of my entire program, I immediately took the microphone and said, "Let's give Bill a big hand for putting together this convention, which will be of great benefit to everyone. I appreciate Bill's very kind words about my books, tapes, and manuals, and look forward to answering any questions you may have at the table in the back of the room."

THE SOLUTION

Many highly-competent people are not comfortable "hearing" their voice over a public address system. That's unfortunate because the purpose of speaking in the first place is to give people information that they can hear as well as understand. To overcome microphoneitis, try the following:

1. Remind yourself that the information you have is important and that as an introducer, master of ceremonies, presenting an agenda or announcing a break, people need to hear you.
2. Go into a room, either by yourself or with a friend, and spend 15 to 20 minutes speaking over a microphone as you listen to your voice. Listen to your friend's voice on the microphone and you'll quickly see that it's just an extension of their normal speaking voice, as it is of yours. The next time you speak into a microphone you should be accustomed to the sound and be much more at ease.
3. Remember to continue to tell yourself that this is not about your voice but the information your listeners receive when listening to your message.

Use this as a guide: if the room is more than a thousand feet square, use a microphone. And if you naturally speak softly, use your best judgment about microphones and room size to make certain you can be heard.

21

WHAT IF MY COMFORT ZONE IS BEHIND THE LECTERN?

THE SITUATION

Sitting in the audience at a corporate annual meeting several months ago, I watched the CEO as he delivered his opening remarks to his management team assembled in the audience. His level of discomfort was obvious as he rocked back and forth from one foot to another. He had such a fierce grip on the lectern that I swear you could see his white knuckles.

To top it off, he read most of his speech, completely failing to share with his audience his genuine passion for his organization and what they had achieved over the past year.

The lectern is not a "hiding place" where you can disguise your discomfort for speaking in public. Instead, it should be thought of as a "prop" that can enhance your presentation and give it a great deal of power. I've seen it done many times and a prime example comes to mind when I think of specific occasions where I was impressed with a speaker's use of the lectern.

Many years ago I attended a political rally where George Wallace, former governor of Alabama and at that time a candidate for president, was preparing to make a speech. His organizers wheeled out this large lectern behind which he would stand to deliver his message. From nowhere, one of his staff members appeared with a box about two feet square and three inches high. Carefully lettered on the side of the box were the words "Wallace box".

Wallace was not a particularly tall man, about 5'6", and immediately following his introduction the box was moved into place, he stepped up onto it, looked out at the crowd, and delivered his speech. He made that lectern work for him that day, and it wasn't just the "Wallace box" that did it. He stood straight at the lectern, used gestures naturally without gripping the lectern for support, and looked out at his audience from his commanding position with a great deal of confidence.

THE SOLUTION

There are those times when it will be necessary for you to deliver a speech or presentation from behind a lectern. Many people see the lectern as a "safety screen" between themselves and their listeners. I see it as a barrier that can deflect the value of your message. If you must use the lectern, then make sure you use it to your advantage as follows:

1. Keep the center of gravity over your feet, not over the lectern. This will prevent you from leaning on the lectern and will encourage you to gesture naturally while standing tall.

2. Stand about eight to ten inches behind the lectern. This will enable you to look at your notes without exaggerated up-and-down head movements.

3. Stand on a small box or platform. Don't become lost to your audience if the lectern is too tall or you are too short. Do not let the lectern overpower you.

4. Unclip your pages if you have notes so you can slide rather than flip them. By placing the sheets side by side you won't have to move them as often. The microphone on the lectern will pick up even the slightest noise.

5. Avoid massaging the lectern or drumming on its sides. This useless noise is very distracting. If you put your hands on the lectern, keep your arms naturally bent; avoid straight-arming.

6. Don't rock back and forth. Because the lectern is

stationary, your lateral movements will be greatly exaggerated. You want the focus to be on your
message, not your bobbing and weaving.

7. Pick it up to read it. If you have a quote to read
   from a magazine, newspaper, or book, don't
   bend over the lectern to read it. Instead, pick it
   up, hold it in your hands, look at your listeners,
   and begin reading. Let them know that this is
   important stuff and you want them to "get it".

8. Don't just peek. Your audience will know that
   you care if you occasionally look at them during
   your presentation. That does not mean a quick
   upward one second "peek", but good sustained
   eye contact.

9. Always seek an opportunity to step in front of
   the lectern (if it can be done smoothly) to
   emphasize a key idea. Your rapport with your
   audience will be increased as you move closer to
   them. Make sure you take the microphone with
   you to maintain a consistent volume. Like any
   other good technique, however, this can lose its
   effect if it is done too often.

While I'm not a huge proponent of the use of a
lectern, there will be times when it's expected that your
presentation will be given from that vantage point. Just
remember not to use that lectern as a crutch, and when
your confidence in your speaking abilities has increased
to a level where you feel much better speaking to your
audience without a lectern, then let it be known that
your presentation will be given without one.

22

WHAT IF I'M MAKING A PRESENTATION TO EXECUTIVE MANAGEMENT?

THE SITUATION

An extremely bright and highly-skilled engineer was asked to make a presentation about the progress of a Six Sigma (a quality initiative program) project to senior management. Having recently been hired by the company for his expertise in this area, he was naturally a little nervous about his first senior management presentation.

While he was meticulously well prepared and had the appropriate visual aids to support his presentation, he wasn't 60 seconds into the message before the CEO abruptly stopped him to ask a question. He answered it, continued on, and within less than 30 seconds someone else asked another question.

He was frustrated, concerned, and somewhat confused because the questions were about the premise of the situation, the bottom line, and not logical steps he was struggling to relate. Completely losing his composure, he began to stumble over some of his responses and felt that they didn't really understand what he was talking about. He was greatly relieved when the longest 15 minutes of his life were over.

As a direct result of that presentation he became one of my clients and ultimately a good friend.

THE SOLUTION

The CEO of a major corporation once said to me, "Dave, I need to know what's going on at the division level and, at the same time, give these managers, senior managers, and vice presidents an opportunity to 'strut their stuff' and defend their position. I try to make the atmosphere as non-threatening as possible but some people are unfortunately overwhelmed, not necessarily by me, but by the title of CEO."

When going "upstairs" to make a presentation, remember the following:

1. Don't be intimidated by the senior person in the room even though he or she may hold a position in the organization several levels above you. While a good presentation certainly won't hurt your career, judging you is not their objective. They want information. Give it to them in a succinct, professional fashion.

2. Give them the bottom line first, the XYZ of your presentation, as opposed to "once upon a time" or the ABC. Don't say once upon a time Little Red Riding Hood was walking through the wood when she encountered a wolf" but, rather, say "The Big Bad Wolf ate Little Red Riding Hood – now here are three things she could have done to avoid this situation."

3. From there, mention your three key points, the bottom line of each point, and then begin to unveil your message.

4. Be prepared for someone to say, "Got it!" Regardless of how critical you may feel this point is, or how much "on a roll" you are, that's it . . . stop and move on.

5. Be prepared for someone to ask a question that may be completely off topic. Give a succinct answer, try to relate it to your topic, and move on.

6. Make solid eye contact with the senior executive in the room as well as everyone else. Let your arms, your body, and your voice clearly demonstrate the real passion you have for your topic.

It's a great honor to be asked to make a presentation to the CEO, president, or senior executive in an organization. Just remember that this is one of the very few situations in which your audience may control the flow of the presentation. That's O.K. They may control the presentation, just don't let them control you.

WHAT IF I GET NERVOUS JUST SPEAKING AT A STAFF MEETING?

THE SITUATION

I enjoyed every aspect of my first job, right out of the army, as a personnel assistant at the Corning Glass Works plant in Danville, Virginia. That is, everything except substituting for my boss, the human resource manager at a daily meeting of the senior staff in the office of the production superintendent. One by one we would go around the room and, beginning with melting, then forming, etc., process by process, all the way through shipping, each department head would present his report. The personnel department was a "stepchild", a necessary evil in those days, so we were always given the last slot.

Harry Tiglio, melting department head and savvy production man with a great sense of humor, was always the first to speak. He had a charming way of looking at life, business, and his department from a humorous as well as a serious side. Invariably, early in his presentation he would throw out a funny one liner which, in retrospect, placed everyone at ease.

During this one particular meeting, however, there was little laughter. Times were tough and some difficult choices had to be made, many of which would be handled directly by our department. I sat there knowing my time to speak was quickly approaching, feeling totally petrified, having no idea what I was going to say. I was so focused on my nervousness that I barely heard the conversation around me. Then it was my turn.

I stumbled, stammered, mumbled, and bumbled my way through the presentation. If it hadn't been for Harry and his reassuring eye contact, I would probably still be there babbling away. I left the meeting and remained totally ineffective for the remainder of the day.

THE SOLUTION

Nervousness or anxiety in a small business staff meeting can make you come across as weak. Regardless of how well versed you are at what you do, if you can't communicate it effectively then you can expect the perception of others to be less than you desire.

I had the problem . . . here are some of the ways I handled it:

1. When a lot of clever one liners are being thrown around, and others are using humor, I have found that if you laugh or if you make a comment of your own (it doesn't necessarily have to be humorous), you will feel a great sense of relaxation wash over you.

2. Acknowledge the person immediately preceding your presentation as they give their report. Ask them a question, clarify a point, or if you support everything they're saying, look them in the eye and nod your head as you listen intently. This will help reduce some of your tension.

3. If seated, and it's appropriate, stand up and use some sort of a visual. It could be a prop, a sample, or perhaps you can visually enhance your explanation by writing something relevant on a flip chart, white board, or even a sheet of paper that you can hold up and show to everyone.

4. Very quietly, to yourself, so that no one else is obviously aware, take several deep breaths. This will increase the flow of oxygen to your brain and relax your body.

It's about confidence . . . confidence in who you are, what you do, and how important it is to every member of your team. It's not about you and what you have to say . . . it's about them and how they will move more closely toward their goals with your vital information.

Early in my career I employed these techniques and was surprised that as I became more confident I also recognized that my job and what I had to say were equally important. My nagging jitters just melted away.

CHAPTER
24

WHAT IF I'M MAKING A PRESENTATION TO A DECISION-MAKING COMMITTEE?

THE SITUATION

A high-profile construction company was finding it more and more challenging to be chosen by a selection committee to build large, public projects. After all, they were one of the biggest, the best (isn't everybody?), had built many schools, hospitals, and municipal buildings in the state, and always completed the project on time and under budget.

They needed to make a change. They needed to do something different so they called me. After 14 intense hours of design, preparation, and rehearsal, they were ready.

Addressing the committee, the project superintendent, speaking to a list of "red flags", said the following: "One of the biggest red flags is the surrounding neighborhood. Noise, traffic, and dust are a significant disruption to their way of life. In the past, we've mailed flyers to residents, but they seemed to get lost, thrown away, or forgotten. The bottom line is that flyers just don't work."

He went on to say, "Now we walk through the neighborhood, meet the neighbors personally, and hand each one a flyer. One day I received a call from a gentleman who worked the 11 p.m. to 7 a.m. shift for his company. The noise made by our morning concrete pours was keeping him from going to sleep at 8 a.m. The superintendent agreed to see what he could do, then call him back."

Calling the man back 30 minutes later, as he had agreed, he told him that the concrete pours would be complete by 8 a.m., giving him an opportunity to get to sleep peacefully. The man thanked him and was not heard from again.

The team members told other similar, personal stories, the selection committee was extremely impressed with their qualifications, and they won the project.

THE SOLUTION

Your listeners really don't care who you are or what you've done until they know that you really care about them, their needs, and their concerns.

1. Tell them a story or give them an example to validate who you are and what you have done.
2. Take the story deep, to the lowest, most intimate level possible. Two individuals, a project superintendent and a man trying to get some sleep. Your listeners will quickly identify with each individual.
3. It's not what is real that is important, but that which your listener perceives to be real. By telling that one story, the committee is extremely confident that every single neighbor in that community will be well cared for.
4. This sets up the perfect question for the committee members to ask competitive teams who follow you. In this case, question: "How will you handle challenges in the neighborhood?" Answer: "We'll send out flyers like we always do."

   Next question: "How effective do you find that to be?" Answer: "It works just fine."
5. Tell stories about what you do, how well you do it, and what the specific results have been, and you will set your competition up for questions they can't answer to the committee's satisfaction.
6. Tell your stories and give your examples with conviction, commitment, and passion.

7. Take the opportunity to use the six magic words of selling: "What This Means to You Is . . ." The benefit statement that follows will capture the attention of your listeners.

The objective of your presentation is to manage the perceptions of your listeners. Do that and you have taken one giant step toward your objective.

25

WHAT IF MY LISTENERS HAVE A HIDDEN AGENDA?

THE SITUATION

A general contractor and his team were making a presentation to a selection committee, the objective of which was to verbally explain their written proposal to build an addition on a current hospital. The presentation went very well, but some of the questions asked by the committee were obviously designed to point out any serious weakness in their concept, corner the presenter, and undermine the project. They found themselves stumbling through answers to questions that were not only unrelated to the proposal, but unrelated to the entire project itself. They were subsequently advised that another firm had been awarded the project.

While the expressed reasons for rewarding the contract to another firm were vague at best, it became obvious that the presenters had been facing a hidden agenda. The committee had already decided on the company that would build this project before the presentation. The subsequent meetings were merely held to justify the appropriate completion of the selection interview process.

THE SOLUTION

Questions that arise from a desire to undermine your credibility by making you appear ill-informed and unprepared can blindside your presentation if you aren't careful. Since you can't know what the "real motives" are, you should prepare as follows:

1. Don't just practice your presentation but also develop and practice answers to questions you might possibly be asked.
2. Use powerful personal stories, examples, and analogies to hammer home your responses.
3. Try to determine what's really happening. The questions, for example, that have little to do with your presentation may be an attempt by a listener to show off. Someone who is trying to impress his boss may seize the opportunity to do so with difficult, challenging questions.

Every presenter competing for a project at one time or another will become part of someone's hidden agenda. If you're on the negative side, stand your ground and do your absolute best. If you're on the positive side, have fun and, likewise, do your absolute best.

CHAPTER
26

WHAT IF I'M ASKED A QUESTION MID-WAY THROUGH MY PRESENTATION?

THE SITUATION

As I sat in the audience watching a young marketing manager deliver a presentation to the sales force, I was struck by how poised and confident he appeared to be. And although he was somewhat vague during his message, some of the marketing ideas he put forth seemed to have merit.

Mid-way through the presentation, a salesman sitting toward the rear of the room raised his hand and asked a question. It was a good question, but one that was more related to sales than marketing. Though quick to respond, the marketing manager apparently failed to grasp the essence of the question, prompting two more salespeople to raise their hands. Convinced that he had the attention of the group, he eagerly answered these questions, only to be faced with several more.

His presentation was suffering a slow death, and he was unwittingly helping to bury it. Having answered all of their questions, he finally jumped back to his original message. The problem: His message now had absolutely no relationship to the conversation which had taken place over the past 15 minutes. So, of course, he got another round of questions to which he again began providing answers. Fortunately, the vice-president of marketing recognized the problem, stepped in, and cleaned up the mess.

This was not an intentional sabotage of one individual's presentation but, rather, an honest reaction to marketing oriented terms and phrases. Instead of being sales-driven so that the listeners could identify with the concepts, it was all about marketing.

Kudos to the individuals in the sales force who understood their role in the organization and stepped forward to ask questions to get the information they needed.

THE SOLUTION

Look at is as a sign of encouragement when asked a question during your presentation. Questions indicate an interest in your message, and frequently go a long way toward settling nerves.

But when it comes to questions, there are decisions you must make before you begin:

1. Do you want all questions held until the end of your presentation? If so, let them know early in your presentation in order to minimize interruptions.

2. Make sure the message you are delivering is consistent with your audience's ability to understand and process what you are saying. Interruptive questions asked during the presentation are often a bold move on the part of the questioner and usually require some form of clarification.

3. Questions may relate to something you plan to say later in your presentation. Let them know that and encourage them to ask the question again at the conclusion if they feel you have failed to effectively address their concern.

4. Accept questions at the end with enthusiasm then give clear and concise answers. Remember that the perception at this point is that your presentation is over. Long-winded answers may make those who have no questions uncomfortable and fidgety.

5. Are you getting questions relevant to only one or two people in the audience? Offer to answer them in more detail after the meeting is over.

You must determine at the outset of your presentation how you will handle questions or comments from your listeners. When you do get questions mid-way through your presentation, ask yourself questions like, "What am I overlooking?", "What points am I not making clear?", "What side agenda could they have?", and "What kind of ripple effect can I expect once the question has been answered?"

Determine up front how you want your message to play out and proceed accordingly.

27

WHAT IF I DON'T KNOW WHO TO LOOK AT?

THE SITUATION

As vice president of sales with the former Charles of the Ritz Group, I had a memorable presentation experience with Walgreens. I got a huge wake-up call concerning eye contact.

On a beautiful June day in Chicago we were making our Christmas presentation, the acceptance of which would amount to 40 percent of our annual business with Walgreens. We were well prepared. In addition to the six members of the Walgreens buying team, we were pleasantly surprised when the senior vice president and general merchandise manager walked in and joined us. We were having a good year and I was thrilled with the opportunity to "toot our horn" loud and strong.

Delivering the presentation at my absolute persuasive best, I made certain that the vice president would not miss a single one of my golden words. I gave him a full 80 percent of my eye contact and spread the other 20 percent haphazardly among the remaining seven buyers. We left the meeting feeling great, patting ourselves on the back, and celebrated with a fine dinner at one of my favorite restaurants.

A couple weeks later we received a large, thick envelope from Walgreens. With great anticipation I ripped it open, pulled out the order sheets, and was shocked when I looked at the numbers. I did a double-take. The order was less than 70 percent of what we had suggested, 10 percent below the previous year's comparable order.

THE SOLUTION

After a lot of thought, I realized I had given too much of my energy – and eye contact – to one person in that meeting. I learned that eye contact with everyone is essential if you expect any success at all as a presenter:

1. Everyone, regardless of their place in the hierarchy, should receive equal eye contact.
2. In today's fast-paced world, no one attends a meeting without a definite purpose for being there. By failing to look each person in the eye, you diminish their importance, which may ultimately impact your outcome.

3. Give good, sustained eye contact to each participant . . . not just a fleeting glance.

4. Finish the last couple paragraphs of your presentation by looking at one or two listeners rather than looking down or at a visual aid in preparation for the next part of your message.

5. When speaking to a large group, in an auditorium for instance, where it is difficult to make eye contact with each individual, direct your focus to specific sections from front to back and side to side. If during the presentation you do nothing else, make sure you give good eye contact. At minimum you'll be giving your audience some indication that you care about them.

Good eye contact with all of your listeners will carry you a long way in any presentation.

28

WHAT IF THE DECISION MAKER CAN'T ATTEND?

THE SITUATION

It was my first week as a salesman . . . in fact I was considered a "trainee". I hadn't yet even achieved the distinction of being referred to as a "salesman".

During that first week, I made a presentation to a client where the decision maker could not attend. I nailed it! I was feeling good about myself until I was advised that my proposal would be discussed with the decision maker and they would "get back to me".

Well, I learned a lot that week. People don't get back to you, you get back to them. I also learned that failure to make the presentation to the decision maker can have surprisingly unpredictable results. Why? A number of other factors enter into the equation: the ability of the buyer to sell my idea to the decision maker, the relationship that I was able to establish with the buyer, the relationship the buyer has with the decision maker, the economy, the weather, and actually the mood of any two people at any given time. And so on . . .

What kind of order did I get from that brilliant presentation you ask? The decision maker rejected 70 percent of the items selected by the buyer. It was a shocking wake-up call.

THE SOLUTION

For the most part it's a painful waste of time to make a presentation without the ultimate decision maker in attendance.

Here are some factors to consider:

1. What is the authority level of the senior person in the room? With a multitude of management layers removed from most organizations today, many smaller decisions are frequently made at a lower level while the big ones "go upstairs".

2. Most of us leave behind brochures, letters, materials, and directions to Web sites that in all probability will never be seen by the absent decision maker.

3. Ask yourself these questions:

    a. "How strong is my relationship with the buyer/committee?" All it takes is one person who doesn't like you to "kill it".

    b. "How strong is the relationship of the

buyer/committee with the decision maker?" Facing many issues, an overworked decision maker may dismiss your concept in a flash.

c. "How capable is the buyer/committee at presenting your ideas to the decision maker?" Nobody really has the genuine passion and interest that you do for your ideas and concepts.

4. If you're in a competitive situation and the decision maker attends their presentation but can't attend yours, definitely try to reschedule.

5. If you're not in a competitive situation and the decision maker is not there, try to reschedule.

The bottom line: unless it is logistically, financially, or otherwise completely unavoidable, do everything you can to reschedule.

29

WHAT IF MY AUDIENCE SIMPLY DOESN'T CARE?

THE SITUATION

Attorneys from a major corporation attended one of my Advanced Legal Presentation Skills workshops. Their "clients" were employees in their division. They addressed such topics as intellectual property, patent acquisition, labor relations, as well as a variety of other legal consultations. All pretty boring stuff . . . unless, of course, you happen to be a lawyer.

Several of these attorneys shared an amazing story with me. When they spoke to various management groups, no one listened. Many of these managers showed up at these meetings with their e-mail downloaded into their laptop computers, prepared to spend the next several hours accomplishing something that was "important" . . . reading and answering their e-mail. What was even more amazing – these attorneys admitted that they themselves responded to e-mails during management presentations in which they were audience members!

The managers were bored, not only with the legalese jargon, but the dull manner in which it was presented. Time is precious to these overworked managers, and they were too bright not to use it to their greatest advantage. Although attendance was required, listening to a boring presentation wasn't.

We devised a very creative strategy which one of the attorneys agreed to try in a one-hour presentation he was scheduled to conduct at the end of the week. His opening remarks went something like this: "I see you all have your laptops with you, prepared to take notes . . . or, could it be that perhaps you've downloaded your e-mail and are readying to accomplish something of real importance during the next hour. Hey! I've been there. I've done that. I rarely miss a chance to catch up on my e-mails during a boring presentation that I perceive has little value to me. I'd like to ask you to do one thing for me today. Close your laptops and give me your undivided attention for ten minutes. If, at the end of that ten minutes, you aren't thoroughly convinced that the information I have to share with you is more important than responding to your e-mail, then open those laptops and go to it with my blessing."

He opened with two stories, both true, both rather frightening, both with devastating, career-destroying endings. Not a laptop was opened and for the next 50 minutes he had their complete, undivided attention.

THE SOLUTION

The people in your audience are extremely busy people. Committed to their profession, they unavoidably find themselves working long hours. They must prioritize their work so when they come to meetings, they have a decision to make: "What's most important to me? Listening to this boring speaker from whom I'll gain nothing? Or, pushing through my 110 e-mail messages so I can get something done?"

1. People will listen if you show them the WIIFM, What's In It For Me? The two WIIFMs that motivate people to follow your message are: they want to "look good", and they want to minimize the risk of a bad decision. The attorney was crystal clear about the WIIFM and how to avoid a knee-jerk, career-ending decision.

2. Before you begin to design your presentation, ask yourself three simple questions: "What is the objective of this presentation?" "When it's over, how do I want my listeners to be different?" and "What action do I want them to take?"

3. Forget the old, tired openings, "Thank you for inviting me" or "I'm happy to be here today", when, in fact, you're not happy to be here today and they're not happy to be here today. So, jump

into the presentation with an opening that grabs their attention, opens their eyes, and challenges them, step by step throughout the presentation.

4. Tell stories, use examples and anecdotes to help them understand your concept. People don't learn from the "technical" information you throw at them, but from the examples that compare one thing to another; e.g., "We had over a thousand documents to review. If we were to lay them all out, they would cover more than two football fields."

5. Mention the obvious (laptops with downloaded e-mail) and tell them an "I hope that never happens to me" type of story.

Don't waste their time and don't waste your time. Maybe the best way to reach them is to send them an e-mail. At least you know they'll probably find time to read it.

CHAPTER

30

WHAT IF PEOPLE START TO WHISPER TO EACH OTHER?

THE SITUATION

I was sitting in a presentation being delivered by a quality control manager to a group of 13 people. It was a highly complex presentation and he certainly wasn't missing any opportunity to pound away at each and every technical point possible.

It became obvious that he was losing the participants, particularly when a conversation in low whispered tones broke out between two of them. Trying to ignore them, he plodded onward, but you could see that he was distracted. On two occasions he briefly paused and, with an indignant look on his face, glared at them. The whispering stopped and started, stopped and started, when finally he lost his cool and said, "I don't know what you guys think is so important that you can't wait to talk about it when this meeting is over, but I'm telling you now that I don't want to hear another word. Shut up!"

Everyone was shocked; they froze, nobody moved. And no one said another word, no one whispered, and when offered a Q & A session at the end of the presentation, nobody asked a question.

THE SOLUTION

This is a clear case where failure to respect your listeners will not only silence them but turn them against you as well.

On occasion, people in your audience may begin to talk in a low whisper among themselves. Not only is this distracting to other participants, it can also unnerve the presenter. When attention is waning, and other conversations commence, you should be prepared to take action in an appropriate fashion.

1. Pick up or slow down the pace of your delivery. Perhaps it's your monotone voice that has distracted the focus of your audience.
2. Turn down the heat. There's nothing worse than sitting in a hot, stuffy room over a period of time trying to listen to someone deliver a presentation.
3. Move closer to the group. If you're standing at a lectern, move from behind it and closer to the group.

4. Make a noise. Try making a sharp, unexpected noise. People's attention will be immediately drawn back to you.
5. If seated, stand up. This will change the atmosphere in the room, gaining the attention of the impolite whisperers. This will also give you greater energy and vitality, which should get your audience back on track quickly.
6. Use an "aid". I always carry an erasable black magic marker in my briefcase. During my presentation, I look for an opportunity to get up from the conference table and move to a flip chart or whiteboard to make some key notations. (My main purpose for doing this, of course, is to add greater emphasis to drive home the point I am trying to make.)
7. Move closer to the people who are whispering. This is real effective if you are speaking to a group of listeners sitting around a U-shaped table. Merely walk into the "U", briefly stop in front of the whispering culprits, turn around to the rest of the group, complete your point, and then walk back to the front of the room.
8. Mention one of the offender's names in the context of your presentation. There are no words sweeter to anybody's ears than their own name. Be sure to use it in a positive, as opposed to a derogatory, fashion.
9. Ask a question. Mention the person's name to get their attention and then ask an opinion-based question.

10. State the obvious. When the whispering happens, and in a long, all-day seminar, occasionally it does, I'll say directly to the offenders, "Do you have a question or have I been unclear about something . . . sometimes I have a tendency to not explain some of the points I've been making in enough detail." They'll always reply in the negative and whisper no more.

Nothing is more distracting to a presenter than a series of small side conversations among the participants. Keep these ideas in mind, and the next time your presentation is interrupted, respectfully take charge and keep your message on track.

CHAPTER
31

WHAT IF MY LISTENERS KNOW MORE THAN I DO?

THE SITUATION

Very early in my career I was engaged to speak on the subject of sales and sales management to a group of CEOs. Since becoming a professional speaker I have always been comfortable when speaking before any type or size of audience. I have always felt confident in my ability to handle any situation, but this, a CEO conference, a group of high-powered, brilliant, millionaire CEOs . . . I was more than a little overwhelmed.

I thought long and hard about the topic. High-powered sales techniques? Fancy, smooth-toned sales management? Everything I came up with sounded phony and contrived. Then I remembered an interview I had heard many years before with Billy Martin, who at the time was the manager of a free-falling New York Yankees team which had amazingly lost something like sixteen of their last eighteen games. On a scheduled day off, Martin ordered a group of millionaire ball players to Yankee stadium to practice, of all things, batting, throwing, catching, base running, sliding – all the basics necessary to play the game of baseball. The Yankees went on to win the American League championship series and capped it off by winning (so what else is new) another World Series title.

Martin was right. All the strategy, talent, and wisdom in the world are of no value without applying the fundamentals.

I reflected back on the basics and, more importantly, who I really was: a former salesman, district manager, and regional manager, then vice president of sales, and a recognized specialist in turning around floundering sales organizations.

Once I had everything in perspective, it was easy. From there I went on to deliver a meaningful presentation that resulted in the acquisition of a number of new clients, several with whom I have established both strong professional and personal relationships.

THE SOLUTION

Though your audience members may hold higher positions, wield a lot more power, appear to be intimidating, and certainly make a lot more money, try some of these ideas to put things in proper perspective:

1. What seems obvious to you could be important to others. Just because someone is in a senior position several levels above you does not mean that they possess the same knowledge as you do.

2. Recognize that the information you have is valuable to those who are there to hear it. Senior executives want as much information as possible in order to make the best decisions. Make the most of the precious time you have before high level decision makers.

3. If the intimidation factor begins to grab you, sit back, relax, and ask yourself these two questions: "What is the objective of my presentation?" and "When it's over, how will they be able to use this information?" Discovering the answer to these questions will help put you at ease.

4. Start with the basics; build your presentation on a strong foundation. Make sure you support your information with anecdotes, testimonials, and relevant examples. Do not assume they share your knowledge of the specific technical aspects of your message.

5. Time is an extremely valuable commodity. No one wants to spend any more time in a meeting than is absolutely necessary. People are there

because they believe you have something important to share. Don't disappoint them.

Dale Carnegie said to speak about that which you've earned the right to speak. Well, you've certainly earned the right or you wouldn't have been asked to speak to this illustrious group, so muster up your confidence, get up and speak from the heart of your knowledge, and they will know why you have earned the right.

32

WHAT IF I DON'T KNOW WHAT TO WEAR?

SITUATION #1

I was the speaker at a convention of jet engine salesmen held at an airport hotel in Los Angeles on a Sunday afternoon. I was thinking about what to wear . . . jet engine salesmen, an airport hotel, a Sunday afternoon . . . business casual, of course. Showing up in a pair of nice slacks and a long sleeved shirt, business casual, I was shocked to see everyone dressed in coats and ties. And this is a company that, in their home office, dresses business casual!

Needless to say, I felt very uncomfortable and very irritated with myself because I forgot to check out the "dress code" for the meeting.

SITUATION #2

I was specifically told that the attendees at a meeting held in Innesbrook, Florida, a great golf resort, would be dressed casually in shorts and t-shirts. Okay, I can handle that. I showed up wearing a nice pair of khakis and a golf shirt. Fit right in.

The president then asks me if I would like to join the CEO and president of the parent company for lunch. I couldn't believe my eyes as I sat down at the table and saw these two guys on a muggy, hot summer day at a beautiful Florida resort dressed in suits and ties. It was a great opportunity to meet them and we had a spirited conversation during the meal, but I felt funny being underdressed and not as comfortable as I would've liked.

SITUATION #3

I was asked to speak to a custom clothier trade association where I knew everyone would show up in outstanding custom made clothing. Now, I have some real nice suits, but I knew that this group would be checking me out from head to toe.

So, what did I do? I went to one of these custom clothiers and had him make me a brand new custom made suit along with a custom made shirt with elegant French cuffs. It was a perfect excuse to get a new suit!

THE SOLUTION

Over the years dress codes have become much more lenient and casual. There are as many pros as there are cons between various forms of dress and productivity. As a presenter, however, the rules are a little more clearly defined.

1. If you're making a serious presentation in either your or a client's boardroom, you should dress in business attire. That is not a sport coat or pantsuit but, rather, business attire, which for men includes a tie.
2. When the atmosphere is known to be more casual, a long-sleeved shirt and a nice pair of slacks, and for women a skirt and blouse, would be considered appropriate.
3. When you are delivering a presentation at a meeting, convention, event, etc., your mode of dress should be equal to or better than the best-dressed person in the room.
4. I'm a long-time member of the National Speakers Association. For years I never attended a meeting without wearing a business suit and tie. Several years ago it was suggested that we dress more casually when attending the meetings. It was a great idea because you're certainly much more comfortable sitting there in a pair of khaki pants than a wool suit. However, when I am scheduled to make a presentation, I always wear a suit and tie.

5. Business Professional, Men: a dark suit, white or pale blue shirt, contrasting necktie with at least 25 percent red color, shined shoes, recent haircut, trimmed beards, mustaches, and fingernails. Business Casual, Men: dress slacks, dark long-sleeved shirt.

6. What not to wear, men: white, gray, or tan suits. Light colors detract from your face and hands. Yellow, pink, or plaid shirts. Excessively loose or tight fitting clothing.

7. Business Professional, Women: dark suit, skirt cut at or below the knee, shoes with a maximum two-inch heel, closed toes, closed heels, maximum one ring on each hand, simple earrings. Business Casual, Women: dress or skirt and blouse, possibly a dark blazer.

8. What not to wear, women: mini-skirts, three-inch heels, open toed shoes, multiple bracelets (jangle), pantsuits, multi-colored blouses and dresses.

John Malloy perhaps said it best many years ago in his book "Dress for Success". "If you want to work in corporate America, you'd better dress like corporate America."

True, corporate America has relaxed some of its standards of dress, but if you take a quick peek in a closet or behind the door, don't be surprised to see a business suit, white shirt or blouse, and a contrasting tie.

33

WHAT IF I ALWAYS PANIC BEFORE A PRESENTATION?

THE SITUATION

One of my clients, a highly respected senior executive, readily admitted that for thirty minutes or so before he was scheduled to make a presentation, he would get butterflies in his stomach and his hands became cold and clammy. His comment, "My internal organs used to seem to be fighting with each other during the first few minutes before I stepped to the front of the group." He continues, "After the first couple of minutes, everything calmed down and I began to feel much more comfortable with my message. It was those few critical minutes that used to miserably haunt me." He concludes, "Today I'm a different person. As a matter of fact, I look forward with great anticipation to delivering a presentation that gets results."

THE SOLUTION

A human being's number one fear is to speak before a group of people. That's even greater than the fear of death, although many are concerned that both will happen simultaneously!

The vast majority of people are nervous before they step up to make a presentation. It may not be defined as nervousness, but rather an anxious desire to get started, a passion to begin to share information with their listeners.

Cavett Robert, founder of the National Speakers Association, and a highly respected professional speaker, said, "It's alright to have butterflies. The objective is to get them to fly in formation."

Here are some tips you can use to turn nervous energy into positive adrenaline:

1. Think positively. Tell yourself in a positive manner that this will be one of your best presentations ever. This may sound trite, but we have a tendency to get what we focus on. Focusing on the positive is one way to reach your comfort zone.

2. Select three pleasant faces. Depending on a number of factors, your listeners will exhibit a variety of facial expressions, body postures, and overall general interest as you prepare to speak. Seek out three pleasant faces, three people who

are smiling and appear to be interested, and begin with them. Look into their eyes, gather energy from their positive response to you, then begin your presentation. After spending a few seconds with these pleasant faces, move on to the rest of the group. Don't let negative expression rattle you.

3. Take three deep breaths. Just before you're ready to deliver your presentation, take three deep breaths. As you breathe in, count slowly from one to eight; feel the air as it fills your diaphragm, then your chest. Then, again to the count of eight, breathe out slowly. Repeat this process three times and you'll begin to feel yourself starting to relax. As oxygen stimulates your brain, you'll become more alert and prepared to deliver a strong presentation.

4. Practice your presentation. How do you practice for a presentation? Some people like to practice in front of a mirror; some prefer to practice in front of their spouse or family. I find my best rehearsals take place in a private room. Occasionally when I'm in my car I practice my speeches as I drive along the road, gestures and all. I can only imagine how it looks to those who are driving alongside me!

5. Tape your presentation. Try audiotaping or videotaping your presentation. When you play it back, listen for such things as non-words and effective pauses; evaluate your pace, your inflection, and your overall delivery. Be critical of your

presentation but not overly critical. Use it as a guideline to develop a winning presentation.

6. Practice before going to bed. Practice your speech or presentation the last thing you do at night before you go to bed. Your subconscious mind will play that presentation over and over again as you sleep. It won't disrupt your sleep in any way, and when you wake up in the morning, you will not only be well rested, but the presentation will be fresh in your mind.

7. Check out the meeting room beforehand. If your presentation is offsite, check out the room in which you will speak before making your presentation. If the venue is a hotel, arrive early enough to look at the room. In a client's office, if possible, make a point to check out the room, the audiovisual equipment, and anything you'll need to put the final touches on your presentation.

   Best-case scenario, take the opportunity to practice in the same room in which you will deliver your presentation. At the least, practice with a strong mental picture of the room and you'll take one more step toward the comfort zone.

8. Have a quiet dinner with a calm person. The evening before your presentation you want to avoid any tension or stress. Try to have a relaxing evening that doesn't involve critical, high-powered business discussions.

9. Have clear, concise notes that you can refer to quickly and easily. Don't burden yourself with a lot of pages that could become overwhelming and even confusing during your presentation, not to mention the fact that your listeners could be quickly turned off by the perception that they might be in some long-winded pontification. One or two sheets with some key points will help keep you on track.

Remember that the presentation takes place in the mind of the listener, not in the voice of the speaker. Focus on your audience rather than yourself, and you will find that many of your fears will fade away.

34

WHAT IF I HAVE TO PARTICIPATE IN A TEAM PRESENTATION?

THE SITUATION

Two partners and three senior managers of a major public accounting firm made a presentation to the executive committee of a large Fortune 500 company. They were one of three firms selected to make the final oral presentation to provide a valuable consulting service in a highly technical area.

Everything seemed to go wrong from the start. One of the members couldn't locate the meeting site, plus he had forgotten his cell phone at home. Further, the configuration of the meeting room was such that the setup they were accustomed to using for their PowerPoint™ presentations had to be changed. Normal glitches? Yes. Could have been avoided? Absolutely!

The leadoff "batter", the senior project manager, a very dynamic speaker started the meeting with a great mood of optimism and anticipation. The second speaker, a brilliant man but an unsure speaker, made his presentation in a very systematic, low-key manner. Because his style was so different from that of the first presenter, the mood of the meeting was dramatically changed. Couple that with the fact that some of his concepts were so technical that, without real strong validation, several committee members were challenged to follow the depths of his message.

Recognizing that the mood in the room had changed, the third speaker realized that it was up to her to provide some serious damage control to get the presentation back on track. And so it went throughout this one hour presentation in which one of the partners got so caught up in the Q & A session that his own team members were legitimately asking what in the world was he really trying to say?

There is no question that they had the best solution and could've helped this prospective client move its business forward in a significant fashion. But they lost their advantage. Not because they weren't good technicians, but because they were unable to explain their concepts and ideas in a meaningful, persuasive manner. Presenting technical information is all about explaining your concepts in a fashion that leaves your listeners feeling confident that you can do what you claim.

THE SOLUTION

This presentation was fraught with problems, including the apparent lack of organization, the contrasting speaker's styles, the rambling, and most of all the failure to explain and validate key points. They appeared to have had a complete misunderstanding of the meeting's real objective.

A team presentation requires the participation of several speakers, each contributing their expertise to the overall effort.

To prepare and deliver a team presentation:

1. Team members must be introduced at the beginning of the presentation and the role of each briefly defined by a member of the group.

2. You may have five presenters, but this is still just one presentation. Each segment is an integral part of the whole that must be conducted in harmony with each other.

3. Team members must work together during the execution of the presentation. When one member is covering specific information, other members of the team must be looking on intently. Thumbing through notes or casually leaning back in a chair with arms folded sends a negative message to your listeners.

4. Involve management from the beginning. Frequently senior team members are unavail-

able for the early stages of the preparation phase. Failure to involve senior management on the project may have disastrous results. It is critical that all members are kept up to speed as changes in the presentation are made.

5. Set up periodic review points. It is not only important for team members to communicate with one another to ensure they're on the same track, but all team members should understand the responsibility held by others.

6. Pay close attention to detail! When a pilot enters a cockpit of an airplane, he does a complete pre-flight check of the instruments. Every detail is attended to in order to minimize a less than desirable outcome. The same is true for a presentation. Don't assume that room arrangements, audiovisual equipment, etc. have been identified and handled. Make sure all details are handled prior to the last minute, and that everyone will arrive well ahead of schedule.

7. Rehearse. If there's one single reason why team presentations come up short, it's from failing to practice. The number one excuse: "We just don't have time to get together to practice." Some teams feel so comfortable with each other that they try to "wing it", and still others are apprehensive about making a presentation during a practice session for fear that their nervousness in front of their peers will be career threatening.

Now is the time to make sure transitions have been worked out and that each person speaking will support the information given by the previous presenter. The best solution: video-tape the practice session and critique the results.

8. Emphasize the benefits the client will realize and validate them by describing success on similar projects. Don't get caught up in telling them what you do and how you will do it. It is all about what's in it for them.

9. Drop the industry jargon, or, at a minimum, explain what it means.

10. Rehearse Q & A. Identify one person who will direct every question to the appropriate team member.

Team presentations are becoming more common and generally confront speakers with challenges that radically differ from the traditional single-presenter speech. Much like a baseball team performs in close harmony, presentation teams must do likewise.

CHAPTER
35

WHAT IF I'M ASKED TO GIVE AN IMPROMPTU SPEECH?

THE SITUATION

Have you ever been to a meeting where you were asked to "get up and say a few words if you don't mind"? Just hearing those words causes most people to freeze or start looking for the nearest exit.

I was attending a local community function one evening when, out of the blue, the master of ceremonies invited the Lieutenant Governor to come up and say a few words. Confidently he strode to the platform, stepped behind the microphone, and delivered a simply magnificent "impromptu" speech. Using stories and anecdotes, he had people laughing and completely entertained, as well as informed, throughout his entire 10-minute speech.

At the conclusion of the evening I approached him to compliment him on his excellent message but also to ask him how he was able to pull it off so eloquently. His response to me was that he's frequently asked to "get up and say a few words" so, in anticipation of that, he has mentally prepared several different speeches revolving around themes about which he may be asked to speak. He continued by saying that he has a wealth of stories and anecdotes that he can insert into any of these messages.

Many successful business executives have personally told me that they use similar techniques and are always prepared to "say a few words if you don't mind".

THE SOLUTION

In the course of your career there is no question that you will be asked to give a "spur of the moment" speech or presentation. Getting up to speak without any formal preparation can unnerve even the greatest speakers. You're not alone, but when you're put on the spot you really can't duck it . . .you do have to say a few words.

Here are some strategies you can use when you've been asked to speak spontaneously:

1. Always have a few words prepared in the back of your mind. There is really no such thing as an

impromptu speech. There are speeches that are given on an impromptu basis, but the best of speakers will tell you they always have a few words they can deliver at a moment's notice.

2. Don't panic. Don't let yourself become intimidated or unglued. You may find yourself standing there ready to speak, your mind goes blank, your mouth becomes dry, and you have absolutely no idea what to say. Pause for a couple of seconds, take the time to compose yourself, then begin.

3. Banter back and forth by sharing a laugh or a handshake with people as you make your way to the front of the room. Ever watch the President as he enters the Senate chambers to deliver the State of the Union address – shaking hands – sharing a laugh? Even the most powerful and eloquent use tricks and gimmicks to squash unwanted tension.

4. Stick to one subject. In order for you to remain focused, deal with just one subject covering one or two key points that relate to that subject.

5. Discuss only one or two important points. Don't give an A-Z history of your subject. Take one or two specific points and discuss them in a frank, forthright manner.

6. Don't ramble. The worst presentations, impromptu or prepared, occur when the speaker begins to ramble. Stop and pause between sentences. Think about what you really want to say. Then give a clear and concise presentation.

7. Use stories and anecdotes to validate and support your key points. If you've wondered how a speaker who has just delivered a wonderful impromptu speech came up with a story on the spur of the moment, stop wondering. The speaker probably had the story in the back of his or her mind and was prepared to deliver it at a moment's notice.

8. Give strong eye contact. Meet the eyes of your listeners. Communicate with them and through them to demonstrate your confidence and commitment to what you are saying.

9. Close firmly. Find a logical ending place and close. At the point when you are through, stop talking.

There really is no such thing as an impromptu speech . . . just a prepared impromptu speaker.

WHAT IF I HAVE TO DELIVER A WRITTEN SPEECH?

THE SITUATION

Several years ago I received a rather unusual request. A company wanted me to keynote their national sales meeting, but they asked me if I could develop and deliver my presentation in conjunction with a three-screen multi-media presentation.

Essentially, the challenge here was to read the speech in conjunction with a PowerPoint™ presentation going on behind me. It wasn't my usual way of giving a speech since I prefer to work using minimal notes or none at all, but, with practice, it came off extremely well.

In another instance, I was engaged by the president of a large manufacturing company to deliver a 10-minute presentation to members of the media. Since every word I said could potentially appear in print, I was challenged to prepare and deliver a speech word for word. Fortunately, I was able to participate in the drafting of the statement so I was able to use my own words instead of someone else's.

THE SOLUTION

In your career you will probably deliver fewer than 10 percent of your presentations using a script. In these instances, you will write and/or deliver a prepared speech. The following tips will aid in the preparation and delivery of a manuscript speech:

1. This is still a speech. Sight and sound are still the media. This is not to be confused with an essay on two legs. You are not a "talking head".

2. Maintain your energy. It's easy to become lethargic and thereby come off as dull and boring to your audience. Your passion for your presentation must come through by maintaining your energy at a high level.

3. Use your own wording if possible. You should use your own words and phrases. This will happen, of course, if you write your own speech. On the other hand, if the speech will be written for you, be sure to read it out loud several times before presenting it to make sure the words and

phrases come easily to you. If they don't, seek out ways to change the wording to suit your style.

4. Use spoken rather than written language. Try to avoid writing the speech out longhand or on your computer. Instead, dictate your speech into a tape recorder and have it transcribed or use voice recognition dictation. You will find it is much easier to speak the spoken word than it is to speak the written word.

5. Use short, simple sentences. Avoid using convoluted phrases and dependent clauses that may blur the clarity of your thoughts. Short, simple sentences will give you an opportunity to pause, look at your audience, and return comfortably to your presentation.

6. Prepare the manuscript in large print using both upper and lower case. The large print on the page should be triple spaced with wide margins. Divide the paper from top to bottom in thirds. Your prepared speech will then look like this: one-third left margin, one-third text, one-third right margin. Separate this speech into paragraphs and use bold letters to set up each of your key points.

7. Score the speech. Scoring the speech means to underline certain key words and phrases so that you will emphasize them during your presentation. You can also draw arrows in places where you wish to raise or lower your voice. Avoid using a yellow highlighter. In many situations

the lectern lighting will cause the highlighted sentences to blend in with the rest of the presentation. So that you can pause in the right places, insert single slashes throughout each sentence where the natural pause or inflection would occur. Place a double slash at the end of each sentence and a triple slash at the end of each paragraph.

8. Practice the speech. It's important that you practice the speech, but don't become too mechanical. Practice glancing down and picking up the words and phrases you wish to use and then looking at your listeners to deliver them.

   There is no more powerful way to emphasize your passion and to drive your points home than by pausing at the end of a strong paragraph or section. This must be rehearsed so that you will be able to look into the eyes of your listeners as you deliver those last 12 to 15 words. Pause for a three or four count, then look down at your next point, look at your listeners, then continue your speech.

9. Pace yourself. You may find your mind wandering during this presentation or you may have a tendency to read it too quickly. When you feel the pace is just right, slow down some more. As a reminder you might want to write the word "slow" in the upper right hand corner of each page.

10. Maintain eye contact. Here's a typical presentation of a written speech: the speaker reads the speech, occasionally glances up for a brief second, and then goes back to the page. Several seconds later, when the speaker feels the urge to give more eye contact, once again, a quick upward glance is given.

Actually, the speaker sees nothing and thus the speech becomes largely ineffective. Since your speech is prepared using only the center one-third of the pages it is not necessary for your eyes to go from one side to the other. You should be able to glance at your thought quickly by looking down and then look up at your audience.

There's no more difficult speech to prepare and deliver than one that requires the use of a written format. Take your time, use these ten tips, and you will have a powerful, moving presentation.

CHAPTER
37

WHAT IF MY VISUAL AIDS ARE NOTHING MORE THAN EYE CHARTS?

THE SITUATION

I once had an executive from Coca-Cola in one of my advanced presentation dynamics workshops. When he made his presentation rather than using a standard bar graph or line graph, he used a graph with trademark Coca-Cola bottles stacked one on top of each other to represent the growth and projected growth of this business period. This was very clever and extremely creative. And, most important, it helped him get his point across.

Perhaps the most creative use of visual aids today is found in the highly popular USA Today newspaper. Take a quick look in the lower left hand corner in each of the four sections, News, Sports, Life, and Money, and you will see a graph showing distinct relationships between identified objects.

I recall one graph in the sports section in which they were reflecting upon the number of major golf tournaments, U.S. Open, PGA, Masters, and British Open, that various golfers had won. The golfers were represented by a single golfer who was striking the ball, and the distance that the ball traveled was representative of the number of victories. Jack Nicklaus was in the lead with his twenty victories in major tournaments.

THE SOLUTION

It's critical that your visuals dramatize and reinforce your ideas. So when you're designing your visuals, ask yourself this important question: "What can I do to make my visuals so strikingly different that they will make my audience sit up and take notice?"

The following tips will help you create visuals with impact and visual appeal:

1. Unity. Develop one main idea then support and illustrate that idea with all of the data on the visuals.
2. Emphasis. The main point should almost jump out at the audience. Key ideas should be underlined and highlighted in a different color. Use arrows to call attention to notable points.

3. Brevity. Use headlines, not paragraphs. Omit extraneous material. This is a visual AID, not a visual speech.
4. Clarity. Be specific and clear; avoid vagueness and ambiguity. Use clear labels, strong lines, and well-defined colors.
5. Simplicity. Avoid information overload! Don't confuse your listeners with more detail than they can handle in the allotted time. Complex visuals or too many visuals will be ineffective and distracting.

Always remember, you are delivering an oral presentation, not a multi-media show. Make sure your visuals are clear, concise, and most of all, effectively support your message.

38

WHAT IF I ONLY HAVE A FLIP CHART TO USE?

THE SITUATION

In a small, customized presentation skills workshop I requested a flip chart and an easel. It arrived just prior to the beginning of the session. This easel would have been great if we were displaying artwork at a Sunday afternoon fair. It was not designed to hold a flip chart. We taped the chart to the easel; it came apart. We placed a stiff board under the paper but it caused the easel to collapse. We were starting to look like a broken down comedy act up there!

THE SOLUTION

Flip charts are most useful in smaller rooms with a smaller audience. They allow you to control the focus and they encourage personal style. You can emphasize or develop key points by varying the size and color of words and figures. By using two charts you can post your objectives on one then develop your ideas on another. This will help your listeners stay on track more easily. Here are more practical "rules and regulations" for flip chart use:

1. Be sure the flip chart is supported on a strong easel. You have enough to coordinate without being challenged by a flimsy easel.
2. Use a flip chart to change the focus in the meeting room. If seated, stand up and use a flip chart to reinforce the idea you are discussing.
3. Always carry a magic marker in your briefcase so you are prepared at a moment's notice to use a flip chart.
4. Write boldly, clearly, and in large letters. When preparing a chart, write on every other page as the ink tends to bleed through the paper. Staple the extra blank pages for smooth page turning.
5. Emphasize key ideas with different colors. Use primary colors, e.g. black and blue. Use lighter colors, red and green, as highlights.
6. Check the markers or bring new markers to ensure high quality visuals.
7. Never leave the cap off a marker when it is not in use.

8. Remember this is a visual AID. Talk to your listeners, not to the chart.

Contrary to popular opinion, flip charts are not dinosaurs. They don't "plug in" and don't use electricity. They can't crash at the last minute. I recently had a client who conducted a powerful presentation using a flip chart as her only visual aid. This presentation secured a large business contract and impacted the firm's revenue significantly. As a result, this client was promoted to an executive position. So, when the opportunity presents itself, grab a flip chart and make your point!

39

WHAT IF OVERHEAD TRANSPARENCIES ARE WHAT MY COMPANY USES?

THE SITUATION

Early in my speaking career, I arrived an hour before a meeting and everything checked out perfectly. As the attendees were coming into the room, executives from the company were performing last-minute preparations for their presentations.

Someone had turned the overhead projector on and walked away from it. The president of the company, a rather short gentleman, turned the projector off, grabbed it by the neck, and placed it rather abruptly on the floor. He wanted to be able to see his audience clearly.

When it came time for my presentation, not one but both bulbs were damaged, thus rendering the overhead projector useless. Not only did the facility not have extra bulbs, but this was the only overhead projector in "working condition". Further, this was a Sunday morning, and no stores were open at the time. So I had to make a quick adjustment.

Securing a flip chart from the hotel staff, I drew my visuals on the chart, and from that point everything went smoothly.

THE SOLUTION

One of the biggest advantages to using an overhead projector over a flip chart is that it can be used well with large audiences. This medium can control audience focus, but it can also be a distraction. Here are ways to use an overhead projector as a visual aid:

1. Transparencies can be easily developed on your PC. Prepare in advance; use large lettering and bold graphics.

2. Before your meeting, check your projector, adjust the focus, and center the image on the screen. Tape the bottom edge to mark the fit of the transparency on the machine.

3. Test the machine to see how much light you will need in the room. Make sure you have an extra bulb and know how to change it quickly. Never assume everything will work perfectly.

4. Place a cardboard or plastic border around the visual to manage problems with static electricity. The cardboard transparency border will also offer you an additional place to jot down a few notes.
5. When gesturing to the visual point to the screen, not the overhead projector.
6. Place the transparency on the projector at the exact moment you begin to discuss relevant information. If you display the visual before you are ready to talk about it, your listeners will become confused or distracted by what they see and its relationship to what they hear.
7. Briefly describe all the information on the chart so that your listeners are not left dangling as they struggle to figure out the relationship between your presentation and the visual.
8. Be aware of your physical position, the location of the projector, and how your listeners' field of vision might be impacted.

Just a few cautions from the wise about the use of overhead projectors:
1. Using transparencies requires practice and potentially some back and forth juggling.
2. Static electricity, particularly in the winter, will cause transparencies without borders to "skate" on the projector.
3. The overhead projector makes an audible noise. Those with who are soft-spoken must take steps so they're in coordination, not competition, with their visuals.

4. The overhead projector blows warm air. This could be particularly troublesome if your notes are nearby on the table. During one meeting I recall that the projector placed on the meeting room table was blowing hot air directly in the face of a senior vice president. Not only was hot air coming from the projector, but the speaker as well!

An overhead projector, used properly, can help support a strong presentation. One of my speech coaching clients seeking venture capital for his business made a real dynamic presentation using an overhead projector. The transparencies were very effective, supported his points well, and he coordinated the program perfectly. The result was that he received the financing and brought his product successfully to the market.

40

WHAT IF A WHITE MARKER BOARD IS ALL THAT'S AVAILABLE?

THE SITUATION

During a difficult presentation to a tough client, I brilliantly decided to drive home my point by drawing it out on the whiteboard in the client's conference room. I jumped up and enthusiastically grabbed a marker (the only one in sight), removed the cap, and was dismayed when I discovered that this marker was on its very last legs. But then, so was the presentation and this was just another nail in its coffin. Oh well, you can't win 'em all!

But you can try . . . another presentation, another time, another client. Opening my briefcase I whipped out my own marker and hammered home my point. The client was so impressed with my impromptu, on-the-spot diagram of the concept that he engaged me as a consultant to each of his branch offices.

THE SOLUTION

White marker boards may be considered low-tech visuals, but they are commonplace and found in most conference rooms. Their accessibility alone makes them a great visual tool. They're flexible, easy to use, and good for controlling information to small groups.

1. Be sure to carry a non-permanent black marker with you. Never trust the ones on the board.
2. Write clearly and legibly – this is extremely important.
3. Erase information when no longer relevant to your point; make sure you have a proper eraser handy.

Your always-ready preparation to use whatever tools are available to you to help get your point across will make you a valuable asset to your company and clients.

41

WHAT IF I NEED TO REGRESS TO SOME ANTIQUE 35MM SLIDES?

THE SITUATION

I once attended a presentation where 35mm slides were the visual aid of choice. The room was hot, stuffy, overcrowded and, of course, dark. If that wasn't bad enough, the slide projector seemed to have a mind of its own as the slides suspiciously began advancing by themselves. The speaker became frustrated. He would push the advance button on the wireless remote and nothing would happen. Then, all of a sudden, the slide would advance, seemingly all by itself.

We eventually found the culprit: a wireless microphone in the next room was interrupting the transmission frequency between the speaker's wireless remote and the projector.

After watching this presenter's discomfort, I learned to use a "wired" remote control and had the great experience of sharing my trip to Mt. Everest, without a hitch, with several large groups who marveled at the awesome beauty of the Himalayas.

THE SOLUTION

With new technology and PowerPoint™ capabilities, 35mm slides have almost become dinosaurs. Should you find yourself, however, using a 35mm slide projector, here are the rules:

1. Remember that slides are wider than they are deep. Make sure they fit on the screen.
2. Make sure slides are legible and easy to follow at a distance.
3. Use "build slides". (Successive slides which build upon the information of each previous slide.)
4. Use only a Kodak Carousel projector with a zoom lens with a tray holding 80 (not 120) slides to avoid possible jamming.
5. Use a wired remote and advance slides yourself. Wireless remotes operate on radio frequencies and can occasionally present problems.
6. Slide presentations should never last longer than 20 minutes. To stay awake in a dark room for more than 20 minutes is a challenge for anyone.

7. Always have an extra bulb for the projector and know how to change it.
8. Number your slides – just in case they fall out of the tray.
9. Position a dark slide in position #1 in the slide tray to ensure the tray is engaged in the carousel track.

35mm slide projectors are becoming so outdated that many facilities have discontinued them from the visual aids department. If you are using 35mm slides, make sure you have a projector to show them.

42

WHAT IF I HAVE A VIDEO THAT I WANT TO USE?

THE SITUATION

As vice-president of sales with a major watch company, I presented a powerful video to jewelers outlining the new product introductions for the year. Having successfully made this presentation to several high-profile jewelry chains with great success, I was on a roll. So much on a roll that I assumed that when I put the video into the machine for my next presentation the audience once again would be "wowed" by these magnificent watches. But for some reason the videotape machine didn't work. No one in the room could successfully coordinate the videotape recorder with the monitor. Carelessness and over-confidence caused a great presentation to go down the drain.

But, lest you think I did not redeem myself, I must tell you that I did "wow" the Zale Corporation with my strategic business review which was a compilation of videotaped sales activity in several of their fine stores. Not only were we very unique in conducting this strategic business review, but this video of their stores and their people added a powerful dimension to the program. They were quite impressed, and, during a challenging time in our company, we were able to greatly enhance our position with this major account.

THE SOLUTION

Video, used properly, can be a powerful aid to your presentation:

1. Get familiar with the equipment and test it out well in advance; make sure videotapes are cued up to the right point.
2. Integrate the slides, film, or video with the materials so the audience understands its purpose; clearly explain the connection between the topic of the video/film and the presentation content.
3. If possible, take your own equipment to the presentation. Be sure to test it before you are "on".
4. Limit the length of the video to between five and seven minutes.
5. Integrate video clips directly into segments of your PowerPoint™ presentation to really spice up your message.

In reality, video is not really a visual aid at all. Practically speaking, it's a presentation in itself, so make it good, quick, and to the point. Use film or video when the medium can deliver the message more effectively and efficiently than the presenter can.

CHAPTER
43

WHAT IF I HAVE TO DO A POWERPOINT™ PRESENTATION?

THE SITUATION

One of my clients making a presentation using her laptop computer was horrified when the computer crashed very early in her program. One minute she was on a roll with some great PowerPoint™ visuals and the next moment, nothing. Not having prepared back-up visuals, she was forced to explain, in detail, each concept to her listeners. Details become complicated, boring and lengthy; it's much better to show your audience than to explain in detail, so, ultimately, she went well past her allotted time and didn't get the results she had hoped for from the presentation.

THE SOLUTION

Computer-generated visuals represent high technology that has effectively replaced, for the most part, overhead projectors and 35mm slide projectors. Combined with a laptop computer they are easy to use, simple to transport, and enable you to use top quality graphics during your presentation. Here are some suggestions for using them to your greatest advantage:

1. Be sure to check out the computer and/or projector well before beginning your presentation.
2. Bring extension cords, power surge protectors, and any other possible cables that you can think of.
3. Be aware of your setup and power sources and carry the appropriate tools with your computer so that you can connect any cables or peripherals as needed.
4. Carry a small flashlight if you plan to darken the room.
5. Always have duplicate copies of your presentation on disc.
6. Have your visuals reproduced on transparencies . . . just in case.
7. Gesture toward the screen where the image is being projected – not at the computer screen in front of you.
8. Practice your presentation. Be aware of the controls that move your presentation forward, as well as those that are used in reverse.

9. If you use a remote, don't fiddle with it in your hands during your presentation. It's hard enough for your listeners to pay attention to you and your visuals let alone being distracted with extraneous movements.

Some things you must be prepared for when using computer-generated images:

1. Coordination among several technical and electrical sources is often necessary and the failure of any one source can impact the presentation.
2. Resist the sometimes overwhelming urge to place too much information on the visuals. Over 80 percent of all PowerPoint™ presentations are little more than eye charts. Show no more than six lines and six words per line to enhance the support value to your presentation.

People can't read and listen at the same time. It's impossible. Check it out – try listening to the news while reading the ticker scrolling across the bottom of your TV screen. You just can't do it. With PowerPoint™ visuals, less is always more.

PowerPoint™ can greatly enhance your message and help you connect with your listeners in a unique way. But beware . . . don't let your PowerPoint™ slide show BECOME the presentation.

44

WHAT IF I'M REQUIRED TO HAVE HANDOUTS?

THE SITUATION

Years ago I made a major sales presentation to a large Midwestern retail drug chain. I placed the handouts on the table, intending to pass them out at the conclusion of the presentation. As the buying staff filed into the room, one of the senior members approached the stack of handouts and said, "Hey, this is our presentation," and started to walk away with one.

The remaining members said, "Oh Jim, get me one . . . oh yeah, get me one too." Now they had the proposal in their hands prematurely. And you can guess what page they looked at first. Sure, the last page . . . the one with the price.

Next they read through the proposal at their pace, not my pace, and made numerous comments about what was being proposed relative to our company's presence and sell-through in their stores. I found myself altering my presentation significantly. Instead of approaching the sale offensively, I was clearly on the defensive. We got the order, but not without a great deal of justification and a commitment to an unusually high stock adjustment after the Christmas season.

THE SOLUTION

Handouts can help your audience follow the flow of your presentation and will give them a place to jot down any notes. This is a visual aid the audience can use not only during your presentation but afterward as well. Follow these guidelines for handouts that do what you want them to do:

1. Determine when you wish to present the handouts to your listeners, recognizing that when they receive them they will immediately start flipping through to see what's there.
2. Handouts not distributed in a timely fashion can cause lack of focus during the presentation.
3. Distributed too early, handouts may promote the feeling that your audience has all the information they need, and they may even be tempted to get up and leave.
4. Handed out too late, people may never coordinate with notes taken during the meeting, potentially causing the essence of your presentation to be lost.

5. Print your handouts using bold fonts, and make them easy to read. Give your audience a space to write their notes and thoughts.
6. With handouts that are exact replicas of your other visual aids, e.g., PowerPoint™, you provide an excellent take away for them.

Here's how handouts are supposed to work and an example of how they add to a successful presentation: when making another presentation, similar to the Midwestern retail drug chain I spoke of earlier, we kept the handouts in my briefcase and handed them out at the appropriate time during the presentation. We also removed the last page, the one with the price, choosing to give them that particular page at the conclusion of the presentation. We walked out securing our proposed order.

45

WHAT IF SAMPLES OR MODELS SEEM MOST APPROPRIATE?

THE SITUATION

As Vice President of Sales with Charles of the Ritz, I made a presentation to a high-profile department store. For the presentation I carried one each of several samples with me and proceeded to pass them out among members of the buying committee. As samples were passed around, people were all looking at different items while I was addressing each successive product from the head of the table. It was very confusing. It was as if five presentations were going on simultaneously. I was learning a valuable lesson the hard way. Pausing for a moment, I collected the samples and then continued the presentation.

I took that lesson seriously and several days later, when making the same presentation to another high-profile department store, I made sure every member of the buying committee got a sample of each product, one by one, as it came up in the presentation. The result: a nice healthy Christmas order.

THE SOLUTION

Samples are simply models of your products that people can hold in their hand, or, with larger items, can physically observe. Audience interaction with your product can significantly enhance your message, but presenting the samples appropriately is the key to making them work for you. To use samples correctly:

1. Avoid passing individual samples around the room. By the time the last person has the sample in their hand, your reference to that particular topic will probably be long gone, and so will your message.
2. Make sure you have a sample for everyone or at minimum one sample for every two people.
3. Watch your listeners as they handle and observe the samples. Listen to their comments to others in the room. Check out their facial expressions and body language. Awareness during the sample review will provide a lot of insight that can help you make any adjustment necessary to

move the presentation to a successful conclusion.

4. When finished with the samples, move them aside or take them away to keep your audience from being distracted by them.

5. If written material accompanies the sample, be prepared for them to make a choice – listen to you or launch into reading this "new" interesting material.

6. If your listeners start a brisk conversation regarding your samples that disrupts the flow of your presentation, encourage a brief group discussion on that particular sample and then continue on with your presentation.

If you have samples of the product you're presenting that you can use in the fashion I've just described, by all means, go with samples. You will have an appreciative audience and create a strong connection between you, your product, and your objective.

46

WHAT IF SOME SORT OF DISASTER OCCURS?

As a professional speaker and vice-president of sales & marketing for several Fortune 500 companies, I've either witnessed, participated in, or heard about some completely unexpected, surprising situations that occurred during presentations. Listed below are some actual situations with suggested solutions:

WHAT IF THE STAGE COLLAPSES? (OUCH!)

THE SITUATION

At the closing banquet of our national sales meeting, I was speaking to my sales team from the platform. Rather than standing in a fixed position behind a lectern, I prefer to move across the stage in order to make direct contact with each participant.

Checking everything in the room prior to the dinner and my meeting, quite to my surprise I discovered a "mushy" spot on the platform that had been built as a stage. Because I was already late for another meeting I neglected to point it out to the hotel staff.

Fast forward to my closing speech. I'm on a roll, and I inadvertently step squarely in the center of that soft spot. I hear this horrible cracking sound and the next thing I know my right leg is tightly wedged between two of the planks.

One of my sales managers said, "Some people will go to any lengths just to get a laugh."

The hotel staff immediately rushed to the room and, with some degree of difficulty, extricated me and my leg. Moving to a safe part of the stage to conclude my remarks, I felt the blood dripping down my right leg and could see it begin to appear on my shoe. I have no idea what I said . . . my concern was that I finish before I bled to death!

THE SOLUTION

I suffered a broken toe on my right foot and had a nasty gash on my leg. I was reminded the hard way that, as you're preparing to make a presentation, if you see something that isn't right, take definitive steps to correct it before you begin to speak.

WHAT IF I FALL OFF THE PLATFORM? (KLUTZ!)

THE SITUATION

In the middle of his presentation, an unusually active presenter moved too close to the edge of the stage and fell off. He immediately stood up and magnificently recovered by saying, "Make no mistake about it . . . what I am suggesting that you do is a lot more than just a leap of faith."

THE SOLUTION

When you're going to move to different locations during your presentation, ALWAYS know where your boundaries are. And how about his "leap of faith" throwaway line? Many of the great professionals are always ready with a humorous line to recover in any situation.

WHAT IF MY VISUAL AIDS FAIL?
(DID YOU PREPARE LIKE I TOLD YOU TO?)

THE SITUATION

Speaking at a convention in Hawaii, I was scheduled to follow the president of a large jewelry manufacturing company. Ten minutes before his presentation was to begin, he was dismayed to discover that the bulb in the 35mm projector on which he had planned to show his slides had burned out. He was visibly upset and concerned because his slides were a significant part of his presentation.

He handled this in a very classy way. Following his opening remarks, he said something like, "I had planned to show you some slides of our new product line, but it appears that the bulb in the slide projector is not going to cooperate. I know you're disappointed because you wanted to see the slides of some of our new pieces." Then, as he held up an actual 2" x 2" slide for everyone to see, he said, "But I've decided to show you the slides anyway . . . my first slide is . . ." He got a tremendous laugh, immediately won everyone over to his side, and delivered a wonderful presentation.

THE SOLUTION

While visual aids add an extra dimension to your presentation, they also bring with them a whole new set of problems. Don't wait until 10 minutes before your presentation to do your "pre-flight" check.

WHAT IF A FLOOD OCCURS?
(YIKES!)

THE SITUATION

I was conducting a seminar for a group of 24 managers in a Southern Mississippi hotel that had definitely seen better days . . . as a matter fact, better years. I noticed a bulge begin to appear in the ceiling directly above the participants, but since I was so involved in the program I simply dismissed it. The next time I happened to look up, the bulge had swollen to more than twice its initial size. Now it got my attention. I continued on but became more and more distracted as this thing literally grew right before my eyes. Calling the audience's attention to it, I suggested that maybe they should move. They stood up, stepped back, and it wasn't five minutes later the entire ceiling opened up and a deluge of water rained down on the tables, drenching everything, including the participants who were now standing off to the side. It turned out to be probably the biggest laugh I got all day.

Here's the amazing part: about ten months later I conducted a seminar before 250 people at tired, old hotel in Bismarck, North Dakota. I was scheduled to speak immediately following lunch. As I studied the room to make sure everything was in place for the program, I noticed, of all things, a bulge in the ceiling. Is this déjà vu or what? I immediately rushed into an adjoining room where the group was having lunch, and quietly invited the executive director to join me in the meeting room. Working diligently with the hotel staff, we moved the entire meeting to another room and nobody ever knew the difference. (To encounter faulty air conditioning and rotting pipes not once but twice in the space of ten months to this day continues to amaze me.)

THE SOLUTION

Of course, the solution is to always check out the room before making your presentation. But who would ever think to look for a bulge in the ceiling much less even looking at the ceiling at all? I venture to say that had the first experience not occurred, several members of the North Dakota audience would have been drenched, the seminar would have been seriously disrupted if not terminated, and my product sales certainly would have been negatively impacted.

WHAT IF THE FIRE ALARM GOES OFF? (LEAVE, YOU IDIOTS!)

THE SITUATION

I was one of several presenters at an event in New York City with an audience of about a thousand people. Just corralling a thousand people into the room and getting them seated by 9:00 a.m. was a challenge in itself.

Following a great opening act, the Master of Ceremonies was in the process of covering a few general items of interest when all of a sudden the fire alarm went off. Eyes darted around, people sniffed the air, some stood up; everyone was confused about what to do next. To my great surprise, the M.C. chose to ignore the warning and continued with his presentation.

Fire alarm still clanging, I approached the front of the ballroom and quietly suggested to the M.C. that he acknowledge the potential of a serious fire and clear the room. His immediate response to me was, "If we do, it will take forever to get them back in their seats. I'm sure it's a false alarm anyway." He even went so far as to announce that everyone should remain in their seats because this was almost certainly a false alarm.

Fifteen minutes later the alarm stopped. It was a false alarm. He was very lucky, and also very stupid.

Many years ago a fire broke out in a hotel in Westchester County, New York. As the alarm screeched, some of the meetings immediately disbanded and people poured out of the rooms evacuating the building. Others chose to stay, thinking it was just another "false alarm". The fire was all consuming, and sadly, on that day several people who failed to leave the building lost their lives.

THE SOLUTION I

All of us, at one time or another, has probably been in a situation where an alarm indicated the presence of a fire which ultimately turned out to be false. Maybe we left, or, perhaps depending on the inconvenience, maybe we stayed.

I will never forget the night I stood outside a major hotel in Toronto, with temperatures near freezing, as no fewer than 10 pieces of firefighting equipment descended upon the building. It was two o'clock in the morning. I was the keynote speaker at a meeting early the next day, and waiting out this false alarm was not what I needed.

Well, it was a false alarm, and I did lose an hour of sleep, but that was all that I lost. Remember, it's better to be safe than sorry!

THE SOLUTION II

If you are the speaker when an emergency of any kind arises, you are in charge. Regardless of your hierarchal position in relation to the audience, it is your responsibility to take action by immediately addressing the situation.

Emergencies are extremely rare, and in all likelihood you'll never be involved in a situation where your immediate leadership is required. If a fire alarm sounds, get everybody out of the room right away. It may be a false alarm, but you absolutely cannot afford to take a chance.

Now, what do you do if you're in charge of the entire meeting? At the same time you announce the meeting agenda, lunch, breaks, restroom locations, etc., add, "In the unlikely event of a fire, here's what you do . . ." and point out the fire exits to them. As I said earlier, in all probability you will never be involved in an emergency situation of this type, but if you are, you'll remember where you read about it and, more importantly, you'll know what to do.

WHAT IF SOMEONE
BECOMES ILL? (DON'T STAND TOO CLOSE.)

THE SITUATION

Midway through your presentation one of your listeners becomes ill . . . very ill. Although I've been in the audience when someone suddenly became very ill, fortunately I've never had to deal with the situation as a speaker. During a large convention of sewing machine dealers where I was one of the featured speakers, an elderly gentleman suffered a heart attack. The speaker at the time was great: he took charge, dispatched someone to call the paramedics, and cleared the room. I never cease to be amazed at how quickly a good paramedic crew can arrive on the scene just as they did here. They stabilized the man and evacuated him to the nearest hospital. And, best of all, he survived the heart attack.

Another time, as a member of a church congregation listening to one of my favorite pastor clients deliver his usual magnificent sermon, a lady at the rear of the church apparently became ill. I heard a lot of muffled voices as whispering people shuffled back and forth to either assist her or move out of the way. One of the elders immediately moved to the front of the church and apprised the pastor of the situation.

Instantly he took charge and briefly explained that someone was ill and being attended to. Then he suggested that we all bow our heads as he led us in prayer.

With the help of others she was assisted from the room. Thankfully it was nothing serious. In the face of a potentially serious situation, in a calm and cool manner the pastor took charge and handled everything very smoothly.

THE SOLUTION

While the likelihood that this will ever happen to you is extremely remote, you must be ready to take charge:

1. Request that the people in the immediate vicinity of the victim quietly move away. If it is feasible, call a break.
2. Ask someone in the immediate vicinity to call 911 on their cell phone. This is one time I'm actually pleased to see someone in a meeting with a cell phone!
3. Inquire if anyone has medical training. Not that they know how to do any more than the Heimlich maneuver or CPR, but their presence could certainly be a comfort to a victim.
4. It is important that you remain standing at the front of the room. Stay there so that everyone can see you. In situations like this people are often very uneasy.

Knowing that someone is in charge will be reassuring.

CHAPTER
47

WHAT IF I GET SICK BEFORE OR DURING MY PRESENTATION?

THE SITUATION

Waking up one morning, a friend of mine felt unusually ill. Or rather, it is probably fair to acknowledge that he was awake most of the night. He was the featured speaker at a convention that day and felt certain that he could still pull it off . After all, the show must go on.

As he pushed through his message, he felt like his stomach was virtually turning over in his body. Finally he knew the inevitable moment had come, so immediately he broke the group into teams of three or four and gave them an assignment to discuss, then urgently exited the room. Arriving in the men's restroom without a second to spare he immediately "threw up everything I had eaten for the past two weeks!"

He quickly toweled off his face, straightened himself up in front of the mirror, and walked back into the meeting room. Problem: he was horrified to realize that in his haste to exit the room, he'd forgotten to turn the mike off! He says, "The audience gave me the strangest look when I returned, but I simply picked up where I left off."

At the conclusion of his seminar, he was approached by the meeting planner who inquired about the strange sounds heard over the PA system while he was out of the room. Being the true professional he is, he remarked, "I'm sorry. I really have no idea what you're talking about."

THE SOLUTION

I once had a guy tell me, "Hey, I would love to get sick before my presentation so I wouldn't have to give it!" Now there's an idea I never thought about.

Seriously, though, I can't think of anything worse than becoming ill either just before or during a presentation.

I hope this never happens to you, but if it does try this:

1. First determine how ill you really are. Do you have a sore throat or perhaps a stomach ache or a headache? Ask yourself how severe the symptoms actually are and will they keep you from performing at your best? On the other hand, if you have a fever, you're vomiting, or feel so ill that you can hardly move, then you have a much different situation.

2. If you determine that you're too ill to do your absolute best and this is a presentation that can be easily cancelled, then do so and reschedule.

3. If this is a scheduled presentation as part of an event, such as a stockholders meeting, board of directors meeting, or a presentation at a convention, conference, or trade show, immediately advise someone in the group and solicit their help in finding a substitute.

4. If you become ill during a presentation, determine how much longer your presentation will last and your ability to conclude it. If it's really serious and you feel faint, sit down. If you need to depart immediately to the restroom, excuse yourself and go. It's best to be up front with your audience and tell them. If necessary, conclude your portion of the meeting at that time.

5. If you have a severe sore throat and it is extremely painful to talk, take a half a teaspoon full of honey and bite into a lemon wedge as you swallow. You will find this remarkably soothing and it will enable you to go on.

During my career as a professional speaker, there have been a handful of occasions when I was so ill that I never thought I would be able to finish let alone begin my presentation. In every one of those instances, I took several deep breaths, said a little prayer, and when I stood before the group I felt a shot of adrenaline go through me. In every instance I was able to finish, even the three days back to back when I had a fever hovering around 101 degrees.

We are only human . . . we all get sick from time to time. If it happens on one of those big days when you're scheduled to give a presentation, place the focus where it really belongs, with your listeners. First evaluate their needs, analyze the severity of your illness, and then take appropriate action.

CHAPTER
48

WHAT IF I'M LATE FOR MY PRESENTATION?

THE SITUATION

We've all had those wake-up calls that significantly impacted our lives. For me, this is one of those stories.

My first job, right out of the army, personnel assistant at Corning Glass Works. The word was out. One of the senior vice-presidents at Corning, New York, was coming to visit the plant. Rumor had it that this guy was so tough that he actually breathed fire.

The plant was always a clean, safe place to work, but in preparation for his visit it was beyond immaculate . . . not a dab of grease, not a speck of dust, not one blade of grass higher than any of the others. We were more than ready.

I arrived at the conference room 15 minutes before the meeting was to begin so I could get a good seat. After all, in the short six months I had been there I hadn't seen a real fire breather and certainly didn't want to miss this opportunity.

At precisely 8:29 he walked into the room, was introduced by the plant manager, and at 8:30 sharp he began his speech. Not five minutes into his presentation we heard the conference room door open and one of the engineers, a bright young man, entered. The vice-president stopped. The silence was so loud it hurt. Talk about the power of pausing!

His next words were, and I'll never forget them, "I suppose you want me to stop and start all over again just because you couldn't work it into your schedule to get here on time. Well, I'm not starting over . . . you're fired!"

He then proceeded to tell us that one of his purposes for the meeting was to inform us that there would be a 10 percent cutback in white collar management. "And I just solved one of your problems there," he added. You can bet that I was never late to another meeting in that plant, and when this guy came to the plant, I was there, in the meeting room, a half hour early.

While his tactics may have been somewhat harsh, he was an extremely professional man with exceptionally high standards to which he held everyone, including himself, accountable.

THE SOLUTION

Whenever I find myself pressed to arrive at a meeting on time that story inevitably creeps into the back of my mind. Always holding myself and others to a very high standard of performance, I do everything I possibly can to never be late for a meeting. Late for dinner, late arriving to a sporting event, guilty, but never late to a meeting.

The solution seems more than logical, but then why do some of us seem to always be rushing to get somewhere on time?

1. If it's your meeting, your presentation, and you are traditionally late, how can you expect those in attendance to be any different? So don't be late and set those expectations.

2. Get up earlier, leave from your current location earlier, postpone that last telephone call, answer those e-mails when you get back, focus on your objective, and plan accordingly.

3. If going to an internal meeting, plan to arrive 15 to 30 minutes early; to an outside client meeting 15 minutes early; to a distant meeting, i.e., in another city, 15 minutes early plus 10 minutes for every hour of driving time. If traveling to another city by air, do not take the last flight.

I once took the last flight out, and, due to horrible weather in Memphis, my 10:30 p.m. connecting flight was cancelled. I then drove all night from Memphis to Knoxville, arriving 90 minutes before my scheduled 8 a.m. presentation.

4. Mentally evaluate your on-site preparation time. How much time is required to set up your visuals, arrange your notes, focus, have a drink of water, relax? How much time is required to schmooze and network with those who arrive early? How much time to make any last minute changes before the meeting begins?

Whether it's your meeting or someone else's, be on time.

49

WHAT IF I PLAN FOR 50 AND 150 SHOW UP?

THE SITUATION

I was one of three speakers, each of us conducting concurrent seminars, at the Jewelers of American International Trade Show in New York City. Since this occurred very early in my career I had absolutely no idea how many people would show up. Five minutes before the seminar was scheduled to begin, I watched in surprise as people began squeezing into the room, sitting or standing wherever they could. Those people were jammed into the room.

In order to accommodate this unexpected number of people, a loud speaker had been placed in the hallway so another dozen or so people could listen. The energy level in the room was electrifying and the response was great, but I must admit to being somewhat overwhelmed and certainly unprepared.

THE SOLUTION

If nothing else, a packed room clearly demonstrates that people value what you have to say. Here's what you can do to accommodate a larger than expected audience:

1. If you don't have a sufficient number of handouts, suggest that they share. Collect business cards, and when you return home e-mail or fax copies to those who have requested that you do so.

2. Don't be overwhelmed by the larger than expected number of people and suddenly begin focusing on yourself, wondering, "How am I doing?" This is their meeting; they came because they believe you have something of value to share with them.

3. Be sure everyone can see your visual aids. People sitting should have a straight line of focus but those standing may find themselves straining to look around you to see the visual. If necessary, stand way off to the side so that everyone can see.

4. Make sure you have a microphone in the room. If the group is small, you might not use it, but if it's an unexpected sellout you'll need to project your voice so that all can hear.
5. Before the presentation, suggest that some extra chairs are stacked in the back of the room in an effort to help everyone find a place to sit for your presentation.

As you advance in your career, you can expect to be called upon to speak at industry affairs, conventions, etc. Just remember, the larger the crowd, the more people you can impact with your message.

50

WHAT IF I PLAN FOR 40 AND 3 SHOW UP?

SITUATION

I have been involved in several situations like this. About 500 people were expected to attend my keynote address at a convention in Pittsburgh, Pennsylvania. The meeting was scheduled to begin on Saturday morning. On Friday morning it began to snow and didn't stop until well into the evening with a lovely 27 inches on the ground.

The airport was closed, as were all major highways throughout most of the weekend. In a room set for 500 people, I had 46. I moved as many people as I could to the front of the room and those who straggled in throughout the hour naturally sat in the back. The meeting came off well, but the close synergy and bonding you get in a larger group meeting simply wasn't there.

On another occasion, I was scheduled as the morning speaker on the last day of a six-day trade show in the giftware industry. Most people will spend two or three days at a trade show. Nobody stays for six days, as was clearly evidenced by the attendance at my session. In a room set for almost 700 people, five showed up. Five!

I had the convention staff bring in a large table, and we all sat around it. From there we had a powerful, productive business discussion, which was almost a complete departure from my originally planned program but successful nonetheless.

THE SOLUTION

At the outset, this may appear to be a real problem, but there are some ways to make a lower turnout work to your advantage.

1. This could be a blow to your ego if you let it. Forget about yourself and jump right in. Only five showed up. So what? They're there for a reason. Don't disappoint them because you're feeling sorry for yourself.

2. If you have the opportunity to change the room, select one that will snugly accommodate the participants in order to build a tight synergy.

3. In a large room where a hundred or more participants are expected, string masking tape across the tops of the chairs blocking access to the last several rows, forcing people to the front of the room. As the audience begins to fill the room, remove the tape row by row. Get your listeners as close to you as possible. You don't want them clustered in pockets throughout the room.

4. If the group turns out to be real small, know that you have an opportunity to provide them with a completely unexpected benefit. Here you can conduct a meeting with dialogue and participation not possible in a larger group.

5. Begin on time (or as close as possible) so you can deliver your entire presentation without rushing. Those who arrive on time should not be penalized by having to wait for the late comers.

Regardless of how disappointing and challenging the situation may be, there's usually a way to make it work to their (and also your) advantage.

51

WHAT IF A BIG MEAL IS SCHEDULED JUST BEFORE MY PRESENTATION?

THE SITUATION

I'd always heard that if you ate a big meal before making a presentation, you ran the risk of blowing a potentially good message. I'd heard it, I'd somewhat adopted the idea, but my real take on it was, "Hey, that's for them, not for me. After all, I'm a professional."

The dinner was chateaubriand, glazed potatoes, string beans, preceded by lobster bisque, Caesar salad, a sorbet somewhere in between, finished off with baked Alaska, and washed down with a premium glass of red wine. My after dinner keynote I knew cold; after all, I'd given it over a hundred times. I hadn't eaten much all day and an incredible meal had just been placed in front of me at the table.

Now, I've always considered myself to be a pretty good salesman, so I sat there and, without one moment's hesitation, sold myself on the fact that as a professional I was in a completely different league. I happily dug into one of the best large banquet meals I had ever eaten.

Then came show time! Following an eloquent introduction I walked through the audience, jumped up on the stage, and launched into my opening. It was great! I was on a roll. I was going to nail this one! Then it happened: I found myself grasping for words, words and phrases I had said many times before but that night either weren't there or were coming about a half-second after I needed them. For the first time in my professional career I felt large beads of cold perspiration roll down my back. I was literally at war with my body as I struggled through this presentation.

While I received a nice ovation and many compliments from the audience when it was over, I was never invited back.

THE SOLUTION

Have you ever noticed how sluggish you feel for about 30 to 45 minutes after eating a big meal, particularly one that's topped off with a couple of glasses of fine wine? If you're sitting in an audience it's a challenge to listen. And if you have a presentation to deliver, you may find yourself in a wretched war of words. Here are a few points to remember:

1. Your well-structured body has been designed to begin the digestion process immediately following a meal. Instead of going north (to your brain) where it is desperately needed, the blood, oxygen, and energy are rapidly moving in a southerly direction.

   Suggestion: avoid at all costs eating a big meal just prior to making a presentation. The brain can use every ounce of energy that it can get.

2. As boring and undesirable as it may seem, just eat the salad, some crackers, or maybe an apple to sustain you through your message. Ask for your meal to be served following your presentation.

3. You plan to take your client to lunch in conjunction with a major presentation.

   Scenario #1: You take the client to lunch before going to your/their office in order to schmooze, enhance your relationship, and, most of all, uncover any hidden agendas or objections that might be encountered later. Good idea, lots of merit. I've done it myself many times, and often it has worked real well. The negative: certain snippets of the presentation may be inadvertently leaked to the client during the meal, causing them to tune you out occasionally during the actual presentation. Likewise, there's a good chance that both you and your client will feel the effects of the post-big-meal syndrome.

Scenario #2: Conduct the meeting with your client first, then take him or her to lunch. In this casual setting you can informally discuss critical elements of your presentation. Now you can spend valuable time enhancing your relationship and getting a feel as to where your proposal stands in their mind. The negative: you miss out on the opportunity to be tipped off on challenges and objections, but if you are well prepared and deliver a good presentation, that shouldn't be a problem.

In preparing for and delivering presentations, it's not the big things that get you; it always seems to be the little things. My mother used to say, "Wait a full hour after eating a meal before going swimming." Maybe what she should have said was to wait a full hour after eating before giving a speech.

52

WHAT IF I HAVE AN ACCENT?

THE SITUATION

Several clients have come to me with a nagging concern that their accent is a negative factor in their presentations, has hindered their ability to reach their objectives, or is becoming a limiting factor in their continued career growth.

Contacting me by telephone, the vice president of human resources from a major company identified a man in the organization who had great potential but whose career was being impeded because of his heavy New York accent.

A popular politician from South Carolina had a strong southern accent he had always felt enhanced his message. Because they could identify with him, his constituents felt comfortable in re-electing him. Now, however, he was seeking a national office and felt that this accent would not be well received by voters in other parts of the country.

Each of these individuals believed their accent or dialect was going to impact their personal and professional growth. Working with each one, we devised an action plan. Because they were highly motivated, they worked diligently, practicing for hours on end, and each one overcame an accent which was a part of their heritage or their geographical location.

I grew up in western Pennsylvania where I easily latched on to the Pennsylvania Dutch accent. Recognizing that it was a limiting factor in my career growth, I worked very hard for many years and today have proven that you not only can take the boy out of Pennsylvania, but you can also take Pennsylvania out of the boy.

THE SOLUTION

If you feel that your professional growth is being challenged by an ethnic or regional accent, here are some steps you can take to overcome it:

1. Identify specific words from your regional or ethnic background that are clearly identifiable every time you speak. Select 100 key words, then record the proper pronunciation of each on an audiocassette tape. Record each word 10 times with a 3-second interval between each repetition.

2. Play the tape repeatedly. Practice each word over and over and over and over again.

3. Identify someone you know who has no accent, someone who uses the English language in a clear, distinct fashion. Since you can't, in all likelihood, identify all of these words yourself, solicit the help of that individual in completing the first phase of this exercise.

4. Together, take the same steps I indicated above and then commit yourself to some devoted practice sessions. This can be accomplished while driving your car, at home, or, as one of my clients did, on a solo camping trip up in the north woods of Maine. (We can only speculate about what the animals thought when they continually heard the same words being spoken over and over and over again!)

If you have an accent that is impeding your career, take these steps, practice diligently, and you will see rewarding results.

WHAT IF I WANT TO BE A PROFESSIONAL SPEAKER?

THE SITUATION

For the first 30 years of my life I was totally petrified to speak before a group of people. Days, and sometimes weeks, in anticipation of a major presentation, I was physically ill. Stomach in knots, unable to eat or sleep, all I did was worry about the presentation. On one miserable occasion I decided to be proactive and drank a couple of glasses of wine. On an empty stomach, with no sleep, you can imagine how that one played out, particularly when it was to a group of business people in, of all places, a church. And here I was, the plant manager in a new facility being built in their town. I don't recall ever being asked to speak again to that group.

Following other miserable speaking adventures, I finally took charge, recognized the damage I was doing to myself and my career, and through presentation skills workshops, one-on-one speech coaching, and many years with Toastmasters International, I finally became a good speaker. After continued study and practice I entered and, out of 20,000 participants, placed second in the World Championship of Public Speaking. I now knew that I had what it took to become a professional speaker, and from that day forward, I have worked to achieve that goal.

THE SOLUTION

Like golf, bowling, or tennis, the harder you work at it, the more you study and practice the better you get. Becoming a professional speaker is no different — it's all study and practice.

Here are some steps you can take:

1. **Take an acting class**. Actors learn to not only use their voices, but also how to use every single part of their body to convey the precise message they want you to see, hear, and feel.

2. **Join a Toastmasters club and attend the meetings regularly**. The key word is "regularly". Not only will you receive good positive feedback and critique on your presentations, you will also become involved in evaluating the presentations of others.

3. **Be authentic**. Most successful speakers who are good at what they do "walk their talk". Their persona on and off the platform never changes.

4. **Seek confidence and be consistent.** Professional speakers are confident that they can align their actions with their values. They speak not because they are being paid to, but because they truly believe they are changing people's lives. You know you're good when people will pay to come and hear what you have to say and will bring others with them.

The greatest thrill for me is that I have changed people's lives, not just for the moment, but permanently. No one is born a great speaker . . . great speakers are made. Sure, many people are outgoing and have a great gift of gab, but put them in a tough business presentation and we'll see what they're really made of.

So, do you want to be a professional speaker? Do you have a fresh message or a new concept inside of you anxiously waiting to get out? Do you have a sincere passion to help others learn and grow? Then commit yourself to becoming a student of communication and prepare yourself to make that great leap into a whole new world of challenge and opportunity!

EPILOGUE

I chose to write this book in "What If" format because I have personally participated in or observed some of the most challenging situations and wanted to share what I've learned from these experiences in a useful and entertaining fashion. Toss this book in your briefcase so the next time you are facing an important presentation you have a quick reference at your fingertips.

Currently I am writing a new book focusing on the most incredible real-life "disasters" ever experienced by speakers. Have you at any time suffered through your own embarrassing disaster during a presentation?

If you would like to share *your* story, tell us how you handled (or mishandled) your own presentation disaster, please E-mail it to us at speaking@richspeaking.com along with your address and daytime telephone number. If we use your story, only your name, city, and state will appear in the book. A personally signed copy of the book will be sent to you when complete.

If you would like to receive our weekly speaking and presentation tips (typically a couple of short paragraphs) go to www.richspeaking.com and sign up or send me an E-mail at speaking@richspeaking.com.

Thank you,
Dave Richardson

"Many can move a presentation through an audience, but precious few can move an audience through a presentation."

David W. Richardson, CSP

ABOUT THE AUTHOR

David W. Richardson, CSP is a highly-sought-after speaker, speech coach, and presentation strategist. He travels throughout the world helping determined professionals, CEOs, managers, salespeople, politicians, and pastors design and deliver powerful presentations with confidence, conviction, and passion.  Not only does he help you develop and prepare your message, he also provides guidance in creating a strategy that achieves the results you expect.

Dave has written over 1,000 articles for various magazines, newspapers, and business journals, developed 6 audiocassette learning systems and several management and presentation manuals.

Very dynamic and compelling as a speaker, he won second place out of 20,000 participants in the World Championship of Public Speaking and has been made an honorary lifetime member of Toastmasters International. He is on of only 482 speakers worldwide to hold the designation Certified Speaking Professional (CSP).

Contact Dave for him to share his dynamic educational concepts with your group through speeches, customized workshops, or executive speech coaching at 1-800-338-5831 or contact him at speaking@richspeaking.com. Check out his Web site at www.richspeaking.com for additional information.